Soya & Spice

Soya & Spice

Food and Memories of a Straits Teochew Family

JO MARION SEOW

◇LANDM△RK◇BOOKS◇

To Jon and Timmy

Acknowledgements

Paul: For leading this dinosaur out of the cave. Thank
you for everything you've taught me about using the
computer.

Yee Mama, Mama, Ah Peh, Ah Mm and Ah Gou:
Storytellers extraordinaire! Thank you for sharing
your heartwarming stories, your photographs, your
food and your recipes. Without you all, this book
would not have been possible.

Stella: You've filled so many gaps in my memory.
Thank you!

Alfred: Thank you for all your invaluable input.
Your suggestions confirmed that we were on the
right track.

Mark: Thank you for working tirelessly on the design
and layout.

Finally, I want to thank God who has been there
from the beginning. Truly He has made everything
beautiful in its time.

Published by
Landmark Books Pte Ltd
5001 Beach Road
#02-73/74
Singapore 199588

Landmark Books is an imprint of Landmark Books Pte Ltd

ISBN 981-4189-21-9

Printed by Times Printers Pte Ltd

Contents

Introduction

Like my mother and my grandmothers, I am just an ordinary home cook. I suspect that many of you, whether you are a wife, a daughter, a mother or a grandmother, share this same title. While it is typical in most households for women to dominate in the kitchen, some of us are fortunate enough to have fathers and grandfathers who can wield the wok as well. So, I am lucky, as my father and uncle were both formidable cooks in their own right.

I have never had any academic instruction in the culinary arts unless you can consider that brief two years of home economics class in my lower secondary school years as some sort of formal training. I think not, although I will not underestimate what that kind of exposure to cooking can inspire in some students. My parents were my first cookery teachers and our little kitchen was my classroom. I was first initiated into this amazing world of cooking more out of necessity than an actual passion to learn about it. You see, there were six children in my family at a time when there were no electrical gadgets

to help lessen the burden of household chores. My mother had to do the marketing, care for my younger siblings, cook and hand wash that huge mound of laundry for a family of eight on a daily basis. The older children assisted with some chores and I, being the eldest, often pitched in to help with food preparation like washing and cutting vegetables, mincing pork and eventually learning to cook at a fairly young age.

We all have an emotional connection to food. There are certain foods that excite our passion and some that we loathe and would never eat. There is comfort food that fills us with warmth and satisfaction and special festive food that we look forward to every year with great expectation. Food that is part of our childhood, regardless of what new tastes we acquire, is something we choose to continually revisit because this food is, and always will be, part of who we are. The food of my childhood and that of my grandparents and parents was humble and simple, yet hearty and wholesome. Porridge and rice were the order of the day, with side dishes to go with the staple. It was quite homogenous: day in and day out, my grandparents, especially my paternal grandparents, ate simple and unostentatious Chinese food. Their home cooking was passed down to my parents who in turn cooked this food for us.

From my observations of what we cook and eat today, I am struck by the changes that have taken place in the domestic and public culinary scene. There are certain foods that have gone the way of the dinosaurs. I am thinking particularly of *zahb khiam,* those inexpensive store-bought preserved or cured side dishes eaten with plain porridge. Take *baa kee*, for example. It is a kind of crustacean cured with salt, garlic and chillies. When I asked the dried goods stall assistant at the wet market if she sold any *baa kee*, it took her a moment to register what I said; I gathered she had not heard the words "*baa kee*" for a decade or two. Then she actually laughed out loud and said, "Nobody eats that anymore!" I won't be at all surprised if most children today have never eaten or even heard of *zahb khiam*. My own children eat

more pasta than they do *bee hoon*. Our growing affluence means we can eat out more often, feed our children with richer, costlier food, and sample the food from different cuisines as often as we like. Things like *zahb khiam*, eaten by the poorer people of previous generations are gradually and inevitably forsaken and forgotten. There is just no need to eat these things anymore.

Besides *zahb khiam*, there are a number of dishes my grandparents and parents used to cook regularly but were also gradually left behind by time. Both my grandmothers stopped cooking the daily meals when they relegated the position of home cook to their daughters-in-law. My mother, as well as her sisters and sisters-in-law, learned new dishes from each other, as well as friends, from magazines, cooking shows, and cookbooks. When new ingredients like broccoli, *dou miao*, salmon, and pacific dory appeared in the markets and became very affordable, these were served on our table more frequently. When more and more food centres were opened, inexpensive, ready cooked food became easily accessible and so we ate out more often. My mother has not cooked pork porridge, omelette soup or Hiahm Bak for close to thirty years. It was only a couple of years ago that the memory of my mom's pork porridge popped out from the hidden recesses of my mind. I cooked it for my children and they loved it. When I told my mother of this, she reacted with a smile and said, "Oh yes, haven't eaten that for a long time!"

As I thought long and hard, I recalled other such home-cooked dishes that have been consigned to history. These are the dishes you will not find in food centres or restaurants but have been in my family for generations. I feel like I am standing in the gap, bridging the generation of my children and the generations before them.

I decided that I had to do more than just pass on our family recipes. I had to write of the times my grandparents and their children lived in, and when I was a little girl. So, I have written about food that evokes such powerful memories of the past, of intriguing sights, smells and tastes that can, in an instant, transport me to another time, to another place – that of my childhood – when my grandmother, my Hua Mama, was there right beside me, grinding glutinous rice into a smooth paste; or my father standing by the sink, fastidiously shaking off any excess water from the *chye sim* he had just washed. I have invoked for you my past that is part of my sons' inheritance.

If I did not resurrect these forgotten foods and record them, I think my sons and our food history would be poorer for it. My boys and others like them are children of the fast food franchise generation, drawn to certain food by that hip-and-hype factor perpetuated through the media, eating food not just because they "dig" it, but also to appear "in" and sophisticated; all the more reason they should know the humble beginnings of their forefathers and how the food we eat has changed and evolved through the generations.

So, I am blessed that my children love my cooking. Even when they were very young, they were quite inquisitive about the preparation of dishes and would ask: "How do you roast my favourite turmeric-garlic chicken?" or "How do you make Koo Chye Kueh?"

I have shared the recipes for these dishes and many more from my family with you in this book. They are recipes which I have used countless times in my own kitchen to produce food that I grew up eating; recipes that have been passed down from my parents, grandparents, aunts and uncle; recipes that I have refined or modified to suit my family's tastes; they are all variously special, significant or memorable to me.

They are as strong as the elements that draw my family into the kitchen: first, the sounds of chopping and stirring, followed by the irresistible smells. My children come in asking, "What's that smell? What are you making? Can I taste it?"

Finally, this book is a tribute to the special people after whom each chapter is named: both my grandmothers, Hua Mama and Yee Mama, Ah Peh and Ah Mm (my paternal uncle and his wife) Ah Gou (my paternal aunt) and, last but not least, my Papa and Mama. They are just ordinary people who were unafraid of hard work and have given much of themselves in order to raise their families; in so doing they have enriched my life in extraordinary ways. Knowing the adversity they went through just to survive has deepened my appreciation for the life I have, including the education and opportunities I received that were out of reach for them. In sharing their stories and recipes, I hope that others will be inspired to seek out their own roots, and discover forgotten recipes in their families' culinary history. I do believe that every great-grandparent, grandparent, grandaunt and granduncle has stories to tell and recipes to share — if only someone would ask.

Writing this book has been an exceedingly meaningful and rewarding experience for me. To be able to talk to my only surviving grandparent, Yee Mama; to listen to her narrate the story of her humble beginnings and describe the food that she ate and cooked is something I will deeply cherish. Her story and that of Hua Mama have touched me ineffably; I am truly blessed.

Kangkong & Chinchalok

I call my paternal grandmother Hua Mama to distinguish her from my maternal grandmother whom I call Yee Mama. According to my mother, I was the one who coined these names for them. "Hua" was the name of one of my cousins on my father's side of the family, but I don't know why I used the name of that particular cousin. "Yee" refers to my mother's sisters whom I call "Ah Yee", meaning aunty. I doubt there is another family that refers to their grandmothers in this unusual way!

Hua Mama's name is Soh Siok Kheow. She was a Teochew from Guangdong province, and got married and bore two children there. The elder child was a boy, whom I call Ah Peh; the younger one was a daughter, my Ah Gou. My grandfather was also a Teochew.

Shortly after the birth of Ah Gou, my grandfather, whom I have never met, travelled to Johor where he worked on a pineapple plantation. After many months had gone by and Hua Mama had not received any news or money from her husband, she was advised by relatives to go in search of him. So in 1933, Hua Mama took her children on a treacherous journey from China to Malaya. She found him, much to her relief, but only to discover that he was pathetically addicted to opium. The sight of Hua Mama and his children must have awakened grandfather from his opium-induced stupor for he decided to build a house for his family, as well as turn to vegetable farming.

Grandfather found a suitable plot of land in what is known today as Kulai, cleared the jungle and built a house. He dug a well and even a pond in which he reared fish and grew water hyacinths to feed the pigs. Hua Mama was an experienced vegetable farmer in China, so, under her care and supervision, the farm thrived and the harvest was plentiful. They planted turnips, ladies' fingers, long beans, chives, cucumbers, *kailan*, *kangkong*, mustard cabbages, chillies, sweet potatoes, groundnuts and bananas. Hua Mama even planted cacao trees! She would bring the cacao seeds she harvested to the Indian spice shop where they were ground up and sold to merchants who traded in this produce. As for the vegetables, the wholesaler came in a truck to their farm, loaded up the greens and sent these to the markets to be sold.

Life was relatively simple during those years although the work was anything but easy. Back then, there was no running water; every single drop of water used for cooking, washing, bathing and watering the vegetables, had to be fetched from the well. That was backbreaking work! Everyday, my grandparents tended to their vegetable farm,

– pruning, watering, weeding and harvesting. They worked every single day except on the eve of the Chinese New Year and the first day of the year. There was neither leisure time nor activity to speak of but my grandparents were used to such a life.

Despite the long hours Hua Mama put into the farm, she also worked as a washerwoman at the nearby pineapple plantations, just so she could earn a few more cents. She would bring her two children along to the plantation and put my Ah Gou, then just a toddler, into a huge basket that contained peelings of pineapple skin, which she chewed on while Ah Peh played nearby. Hua Mama could then get on with her washing. Once the work was done, they would head back home where she cooked the day's meals and got on with more work on the farm.

Every single meal was cooked at home. Breakfast was a humble meal of steamed sweet potatoes dug from the farm, eaten with freshly picked *kangkong* simply fried with lard, garlic and salt. Porridge was eaten for lunch, accompanied by more stir-fried vegetables, as well as *zahb khiam*, meaning assorted dishes. *Zahb khiam* are usually food that have been fermented, preserved or cured by the addition of salt and/or sugar such as *gong chye* (a slightly sweet crunchy preserved vegetable), *oh nahm* (savoury black olives), salted fish, fermented bean curd, sweet *taukwa* (soya bean curd), *khiam chye* (preserved mustard cabbage) and salted duck eggs. For dinner, it was rice, eaten with yet more vegetables like stir-fried beansprouts (which Hua Mama grew for their own consumption), *zahb khiam* again, and perhaps a simple soup. A much-loved dish was *chye poh* (preserved radish), cut into thin strips then fried with bean curd (page 27). Another favourite was *chye poh* omelette (page 27). Meat was seldom eaten; it was reserved for festival days and Chinese New Year. Then, Hua Mama would slaughter either a chicken or a duck; the chicken was invariably cooked by blanching it in gently simmering water whereas the duck was braised in dark soy sauce (page 25). Dessert was unusual; the only sweet fare they ate was sweet potato soup, and it was consumed more to fill the stomach than for pleasure. Of course they ate fruits, but only tropical ones like rambutans, bananas and pineapples.

Hua Mama and her family lived a largely uneventful life on the farm, except for two occasions: the births of my father in 1936 and another daughter whom I should address as So-e Gou, meaning Little Aunt. I imagine my father as

THIS PAGE: *A typical farm in the 1930s.*
FACING PAGE: *Pickled vegetables, braised peanuts and preserved soya bean curd were the simple fare eaten in my grandparents' house in the 1930s.*

14

a carefree little boy playing and running around the farm with his little sister while the two older siblings helped out with the chores, working alongside Hua Mama and my grandfather.

Hua Mama and her family lived on the farm until 1942 when the Japanese army invaded Malaya and advanced south to Johore. In late 1941, fearful of an imminent attack, a number of neighbouring families fled to seek safety in the more rural and forested areas. Although they were prepared to flee, Hua Mama and her family continued to stay on the farm until early January 1942. She was reluctant to abandon the home that was the result of years of incessant toil.

Two days before the Chinese New Year, or what the Chinese call the 29th night, the farm was shrouded in darkness as the sirens had sounded and no lamps, not even candles, could be lit. Yet, Hua Mama was adamant that they would have the traditional Chinese New Year Eve reunion dinner. She proceeded to slaughter and cook a chicken for that meal the next day. But that night, the bombs fell. In those horrifying moments, as they cowered in fear and heard the explosions, they knew there was no choice but to leave their farm and become refugees.

The reunion dinner was quickly forgotten as they scrambled to pack some belongings like mats and blankets, and strapped a tin of crackers to Ah Peh's back. They escaped on foot in the pitch-dark night. It was only when they were deep in the forest that Hua Mama realized they had left the slaughtered chicken behind. But there was no turning back; they trekked for days without any food other than the dry crackers.

On the way, they met fellow refugees who warned them not to head towards the direction of the railway track as the Japanese soldiers were killing many people there. So they changed their route and finally arrived at a rubber plantation near Kota Tinggi. There, they met some neighbours who, like them, managed to escape the bombing. The workers at the plantation allowed all these refugees to use the warehouse. With very little to eat, they stayed there for the next few months, searching for anything edible like tapioca leaves and roots, banana shoots, and a plant they called 'Indian grass' which grew wild in that area.

During the stay on the rubber plantation, my grandfather actually made a couple of trips back to their farm to check on its condition. The Japanese soldiers had raided it: the pigs, chickens and ducks were all gone. The previously neat rows of vegetables were growing wildly and weeds had sprung up everywhere. He also brought back terrifying news of bodies that littered the route to the farm, filling the air with an unbearable stench. When my grandfather fell seriously ill later, Hua Mama believed that it was a result of inhaling the putrid air as he made these journeys.

Hua Mama and her family stayed on the plantation for a few months until Singapore fell to Japanese rule and things were relatively settled. They then moved back to the farm to the arduous task of restoring it. At that time, my grandfather fell gravely ill. Hua Mama could not possibly nurse him, look after their four children, as well as work on the farm. A distant relative who lived nearby (meaning one or two hours' walk away) took my grandfather into his home to care for him. However, my grandfather did not recover. He died not long after. Hua Mama was too poor to afford a coffin, so he was unceremoniously buried, his grave marked by a simple plank.

More misfortunes were to befall the family. Shortly after my grandfather's death, Hua Mama and Ah Gou fell ill with a mysterious ailment: they were burning with high fever and their bodies were swollen all over. As they lay on the beds hovering between life and death, Ah Peh, then only about twelve years old, had to care for them, mind the younger siblings, work the farm and cook all the meals. Miraculously, Hua Mama and Ah Gou recovered.

With my grandfather dead, Hua Mama realized that she could not adequately fend for herself and the children. Believing that Singapore was a better place to start life anew, she decided to send my father ahead with another relative. Papa was the first person in the family to arrive in Singapore where he stayed with this relative for the next few years. With my father settled, Hua Mama then had to make the heart-rending decision to give away So-e Gou to a Hakka family who lived on a neighbouring farm. This family eventually returned to China, bringing So-e Gou with them. Hua Mama maintained contact with them through the years. I remember seeing a black-and-white picture of So-e Gou, all grown up, dressed in a Mao jacket that we found so strange. She had gotten married and has a family of her own.

Thus, Hua Mama was left with only Ah Peh and Ah Gou. She planned for them to travel to Singapore hidden among baskets of pineapples on a delivery truck. (Malaya was still under Japanese occupation.) They packed what few belongings they had. Hua Mama, being ever pragmatic, took extra care to bring along her Chinese weighing scale by strapping its various components to her legs and body, to avoid having it confiscated. She was already planning ahead to start a business once they reached Singapore. She would sell anything: vegetables, fruits, or whatever she could make to put food on the table. Mercifully, they managed to make their way across the Causeway to Singapore safely. In Singapore, Hua Mama rented a room in what was called a *hai tnoinh choo*, literally meaning 'house on the sea'. These were not kelongs, which were built much further off shore. The *hai tnoinh choo* was nearer to land but a sampan was still needed for commuting to and fro from house to shore. Once they were settled, Ah Peh was sent to live on a farm belonging to yet another relative so he could work there to earn his keep.

Now Hua Mama only had Ah Gou left with her. The two of them eked out a living by selling vegetables and fruits. A short while later, Hua Mama turned to selling fish as she could make slightly more profit from this than selling vegetables. She had to jostle among other fish sellers to bid for fish to sell. They did this by whispering to the wholesaler the amount he/she was willing to pay for whatever quantity and type of seafood. Of course the one with the highest bid got the goods. When

踏车的经验，不

一些骑士也不守

——新加坡业余脚

第22名

政

推广为

具，但

也公路

保障安

安理

马路

席陈

们在市镇内使用脚踏
车，因为这里的交通比
较缓慢，骑士的风险比
在大马路上或市区来得
低。他也鼓励骑士穿上
保护装备，意外发生时

是年长者

样的习惯。"

新加坡业余脚

协会秘书郑则希也

市区的道路并不适

踏车骑士使用。

以他本身在踏

Hua Mama got her fish, she put them in baskets suspended from the ends of a wooden pole that she carried on her shoulders, and sold the fish at the marketplace near Lavender Street.

To supplement her income, Hua Mama sewed fishing nets out of mosquito nets. With these, Hua Mama and Ah Gou would wade into the sea to catch baby shrimp that they preserved to make *chinchalok,* the pink shrimp sauce that is added to chilli sauce and served as a dip to accompany beef noodles. Hua Mama most definitely didn't eat the *chinchalok* with beef noodles. She bottled the *chinchalok* for sale and brought some of these bottles to the orchard in exchange for fruits to sell. The little she kept for herself was simply tossed with chopped chillies, thinly sliced shallots and the juice of some calamansi limes, then eaten with porridge (page 35). They also caught baby squids that were preserved in the same way, but with the addition of sliced chillies and chopped garlic, to make what is known as *gao nee. Gao nee* is eaten in the same way as *chinchalok*, but with ginger strips added to the mix.

Mother and daughter stayed in the *hai tnoinh choo* for three more years until 1945 when the Japanese surrendered their rule in Singapore. During that time, Hua Mama remarried. Her second husband was the grandfather I knew. I called him Ah Gong. He was an immigrant from the Tneoh Ngeoh region in China. The people there were Teochews too but they spoke the dialect with a rather musical accent, as if they were singing opera. Ah Gong had worked as a builder for the Japanese. With his skills, he built a house for the family in a kampong at Mang Gah

Kah in the area we now call Whampoa. After the war, Ah Peh returned to stay with the family. However, my father continued to stay with the relative. He did not go back to his own family until he was a teenager.

Hua Mama, Ah Gong and their family lived in Mang Gah Kah for the next twenty-three years. During that time, Hua Mama gave birth to another son, my So-e Jiek. Ah Peh got married at the age of twenty to his seventeen-year-old wife whom I call Ah Mm. Ah Gou also got

married when she turned nineteen. Several years later, it was my father's turn.

Living in Mang Gah Kah, Hua Mama no longer lived off the sea. Finished with being a fish seller, she became a hawker. She made her own Poong Kueh (Glutinous Rice Cake, page 33), Soon Kueh (Turnip Dumpling, page 37) and Koo Chye Kueh (Chive Dumpling, page 39) and hawked them by the roadside. To make the skin of these *kueh*, you need rice flour. However, in those days, there was no ground rice flour to be bought. Hua Mama had to grind every single grain of rice into flour. To do this, she invested a portion of her paltry savings in a huge granite millstone.

Grinding rice grains using this millstone was hard work: First, Hua Mama had to wash the rice grains and soak them in water; then she would feed the rice grains, a few ladles at a time, into

THIS PAGE: *A hai tnoinh choo built over the sea.*
FACING PAGE, *Hua Mama and Ah Gong on holiday in Hongkong, Hua Mama at Chinese New Year.*

a hole in the middle of the millstone together with some water. She then ground the grains by turning the rotary part of the heavy millstone round and round until a thick, white, milky liquid flowed out; this would be sieved to obtain a rice dough from which she made the skin of her *kueh*. I have fond memories of Hua Mama with her gold teeth, in a half smile, her hands never stopping in rotating the millstone.

Hua Mama coloured the skin of the Poong Kueh a bright pink while the skin of the Soon Kueh and Koo Chye Kueh was white, the natural colour of the rice flour. Hua Mama also made another kind of *kueh*, similar in shape and colour to the Poong Kueh, but this was filled with

savoury bean paste, or *kiam tau sah*. This paste was made by steaming mung beans until they were very soft before mashing and mixing them with lard and salt to form a slightly crumbly paste.

Ah Peh and Ah Mm lived with Hua Mama and Ah Gong as Chinese tradition dictated that the eldest son and his wife were responsible for the care of his parents. (Ah Gou and my father moved out when they got married.)

Still, Hua Mama worked even harder than before. As the family grew, there were more mouths to feed. Ah Mm was an able helper in Hua Mama and Ah Peh's roadside stall which sold fried noodles – Char Kway Teow. Ah Mm not only took over the household chores on top of caring for her children, she also did the behind-

the-scenes work such as preparing the turnip filling for the Soon Kueh. It was an inordinate amount of hard work for the small sum of money they made – just enough to survive on. On a good day, she was content just to be able to sell all the *kueh* she made.

With Ah Mm's help, Hua Mama was able to sell additional food like fried *bee hoon* (vermicelli) and sweet potato soup. All of these food items had to be ready very early in the morning. When the grandchildren were older, they helped in whatever capacity they could, like carrying the food to Hua Mama's regular spot in the kampong and helping to serve customers. In the evenings, after dinner, Hua Mama set up a table outside their wooden house to sell sweet glutinous rice ball soup (page 31) and Muah Chee, a peanut dessert (page 41). Of course, she or Ah Mm had to grind the glutinous rice flour for these dishes.

During the Chinese New Year period, Hua Mama would even grind extra glutinous rice into sticky dough to be sold to customers who made their own glutinous rice balls to commemorate Man's Universal Birthday, which fell on the seventh day of the Chinese Lunar New Year. During the Dragon Boat Festival, she would make rice dumplings for sale. Her dumplings were extra special ones filled with braised pork, mushrooms, dried shrimps, chestnuts and a lump of sweet bean paste that was wrapped in pig's caul. I don't know anyone else who includes sweet bean paste in savoury dumplings.

Whenever I ate Hua Mama's dumplings, I always ate the rice and the other filling first, leaving the sweet bean paste to the end to be

THIS PAGE: *Roadside hawkers sold everything from soft drinks to cigarettes.*
FACING PAGE: Chinchalok & Lime *(recipe on pg 35).*

slowly savoured. It was like having the main course and dessert in one convenient package.

In 1968, the Mang Gah Kah area was scheduled for development into a government housing estate. Hua Mama and Ah Peh's family then moved to the newly erected flats at Bendemeer Road, just a short distance away. There, for the first time, they lived in a high-rise building complete with ready running water, gas stoves and flushing toilets. Perhaps unwilling to leave the soil beneath their feet, Hua Mama and Ah Gong chose a one-room flat on the ground floor by the Kallang River.

Hua Mama rented a stall at the market right in front of Ah Peh's flat and sold Loh Mee (Braised Noodles, page 87) for a while. With the help of Ah Peh's third son, Ah Kuai, she switched to selling Kway Chap, a typical Teochew dish of broad rice noodle sheets with soya sauce gravy and meat.

It was during that time that I stayed with Hua Mama and Ah Gong for an entire year. My parents couldn't get me into a primary school near where we stayed at Joo Seng Road, but they managed to register me in Towner Primary School (sadly defunct), which was quite near to Bendemeer Road. Initially, I took a taxi to and from school but it was too inconvenient; so it was decided that I should stay with my grandparents until the following year when I could be placed in a school nearer home.

I lived with my grandparents in their one-room flat. When Ah Gong woke me up at just after six every morning, the sky was still dark. Hua Mama was already at the market with my cousin getting the Kway Chap ready for sale. When I was dressed, Ah Gong would bring me to the coffee shop nearby for breakfast. We walked past the market. Hua Mama and Ah Kuai were so busy at work, they didn't even notice us. At the coffee shop, Ah Gong ordered toast, soft-boiled eggs and occasionally Magnolia fresh milk in its pyramid-shaped pack for me. My grandparents, as well as Ah Peh, Ah Mm and most of their children were unaccustomed to eating bread and dairy products; the only "western food" they might eat was little triangular pieces of salted butter which were sold at the coffee shop. They ate these in the belief that the butter would lubricate their throat and bring relief to sore throats or coughs.

I have eaten my share of these butter pieces in my childhood. I must say I quite enjoyed them but you can't get me to eat butter in this way now, knowing what we do about its cholesterol content. My father liked to melt butter in his cup of hot coffee before slowly sipping the dark liquid with a golden swirl on top. It was really quite good; I haven't had a cup of coffee like that since all those years ago. The thought of it makes me long for a cup!

In the beginning, Ah Gong walked me to school but he later on, he hired a trishaw rider to send us there. It was so thrilling to be sitting in that trishaw, taking in the sights and enjoying the cool morning breeze while Ah Gong and the

THIS PAGE: *Bendemeer Road flats, and Magnolia milk carton.*
FACING PAGE: *A trishawrider, and a man preparing opium.*

trishaw uncle engaged in conversation. I felt like a princess being driven to school in a carriage. After they dropped me off at school, Ah Gong would proceed to the opium den where he indulged in his addiction before coming to take me home.

As Ah Gong used to work as a builder for the Japanese, he was without a job after the Japanese Occupation ended. So he took to 'cooking' opium to make a living. Ah Gong was a pirate for a short while before he came to Singapore. I suspect his pirate friends were the connection he had for his constant supply of raw opium which he processed into the form used for smoking. He did that in the cover of the night with Hua Mama's help.

Opium has one of the most repugnant yet

unforgettable odours I have ever encountered; I could recognize it anywhere in the world. Cooking opium was an illegal activity; so to avoid detection, Ah Gong used kerosene, another foul-smelling substance to mask the opium's odour. Ah Gong sold the refined opium to his fellow addicts at the opium den. With the government increasingly closing in on this illicit trade and addiction, Ah Gong no longer cooked it when

the family moved to Bendemeer.

After school each day, Ah Gong walked me home. We would first go to Hua Mama's stall where Ah Gong usually had Kway Chap or porridge for his  lunch. I had a choice to either eat at the stall or head upstairs to Ah Mm's flat for her Teochew porridge. Ah Gong would stay to help around the stall while I was free to play or do whatever I wanted.

Hua Mama continued to work until she was in her sixties. When she retired, the *kway chap* stall closed but Ah Kuai went on to operate his own successful duck rice stall. Hua Mama lived out her later years with relative ease, but near the end of her life, she was constantly besieged by recollections of the war. Whenever I visited, she would talk of how her heart would still race from the unspeakable fear caused by events that happened so long ago.

I think of what she was like as a young mother with two small children, making that irrevocable decision to embark on the journey across the South China Sea in search of her husband. If she felt any fear and uncertainty, she must have pushed them aside, put forth a face of courage and come to Malaya.

These recipes from Hua Mama have a special place in my heart; they are for me a testament to her frugality, fortitude and resolve: how she worked to ensure that her family survived another day.

Braised Duck

serves 8 - 10

I have never eaten braised duck cooked by Hua Mama. By the time I was born, Hua Mama had already been a career woman for many years. She seemed to have worked non-stop all her life; the word 'rest' was not in her vocabulary. The food Hua Mama sold, like her Kway Chap, *kueh* and rice dumplings, is the cuisine I grew up on, but, strangely, I have never tasted Hua Mama's home-cooked food.

This recipe for braised duck was given to me by Ah Gou, who, no doubt, had helped Hua Mama prepare this dish. This is basically the way Hua Mama cooked it, but I have made certain changes to suit my taste. I use superior quality dark soy sauce which I don't think was available to her then. I like the deep, rich dark colour that it gives to the duck. I discard the head and the feet as none of my family will eat these parts. I also separate the neck so that the duck can fit more comfortably into my non-stick wok. It is interesting that Hua Mama used galangal as this ingredient is not native to China but is common in South East Asian cooking. I gather she learned this recipe from other immigrants who settled here before her.

1 duck, about 2 kg
2 teaspoons oil
1 teaspoon five-spice
  powder
2 teaspoons salt
8 cloves garlic, smashed
8 ½ cm galangal,
  sliced thickly
2 tablespoons sugar
3 tablespoons of
  dark soya sauce
4 cups of water
4 hard-boiled eggs
Cucumber slices
Coriander leaves

Start the preparation the night before cooking this dish by washing the duck well. Remove the duck's rear end; this is not an option unless you want the duck gravy to smell quite bad. Get rid of the head and feet. Separate and remove the skin from the neck. Although my family doesn't eat the neck, I still braise it together with the duck for extra flavour. Dry the duck thoroughly with kitchen towels.

Heat the oil in a small saucepan and fry the five-spice powder for about a minute over a gentle flame until it is very fragrant. Let it cool. Rub the salt, the five-spice powder and the oil all over the duck, as well as the duck cavity. Leave the duck in the fridge to marinate overnight.

Take the duck out of the fridge. Put the crushed garlic and galangal slices into the duck cavity. Heat a non-stick wok that is big enough to contain the duck. Add the sugar and let it caramelize over a medium flame. As the caramel turns a deep golden brown, immediately add the dark soya sauce.

Let the mixture bubble for a few seconds and then add all four cups of water. Stir to mix the gravy. Let everything come to a boil before putting the duck and the hardboiled eggs into the wok. It doesn't matter if the duck is not completely immersed. Lower the flame and cover the wok tightly. Let the duck braise in the simmering sauce for one hour.

Remove the cover, turn the duck over and continue to braise, covered, for another hour. Transfer the duck and eggs to a plate. Skim off the layer of oil in the gravy. Turn on the flame again and bring the gravy back to a boil; lower the heat slightly and let the gravy boil gently, uncovered, until it is reduced by half. Remember to keep watch; you don't want all the gravy to evaporate!

You can use your kitchen scissors to cut up the duck or use your hands to separate the meat from the bones. Lay the meat on a bed of sliced cucumber on a platter. Pour some gravy over and garnish with coriander sprigs.

Chye Poh with Taukwa

PRESERVED RADISH WITH SOYA BEAN CAKE   serves 4

This was a favourite dish of Hua Mama's family. *Chye poh* comes in two versions: sweet and savoury. The savoury one is for boiling soup (with winter melon and pork ribs). For this recipe, use the sweet kind. My family likes this dish for the contrasting textures and tastes of the crunchy sweet *chye poh* against the savoury soft *taukwa*.

8 pieces *chye poh*
   (preserved radish)
2 large pieces *taukwa*
   (soya bean cake)
2 tablespoons oil
4 cloves garlic, minced
2 teaspoons sugar
1½ tablespoons water

Cut the *chye poh* into thin strips. Cut the *taukwa* into thicker strips as the *taukwa* is softer and fragile.

Heat the oil in a non-stick wok. Fry the *taukwa* strips, turning them occasionally so all sides become golden brown. Remove the *taukwa* and set them aside. Put the strips of *chye poh* into the remaining oil and fry for a few moments before adding the garlic.

Continue to fry until the garlic turns golden and the *chye poh* browns in patches. Sprinkle the sugar over the *chye poh* and stir to coat the *chye poh* with it. Add the *taukwa* strips and stir to mix well. Add the water and stir to allow most of the water to evaporate. You just need a little bit of moisture to coat the *chye poh* and *taukwa* to ensure that the dish is not too dry. Eat with porridge or rice.

Chye Poh Nerng

PRESERVED RADISH OMELETTE   serves 4

Chye poh is a preserved radish that is available in either large pieces or finely minced. A quintessential Teochew food, Chye Poh Nerng is commonly eaten with plain porridge. Thinly sliced *chye poh* was also used as an alternative to eggs as an accompaniment to porridge for poorer families. For Chye Poh Nerng, use minced preserved radish. To get rid of some of its saltiness, wash the *chye poh* first. I believe Hua Mama chose to forego this step since a saltier omelette would have better served her frugal lifestyle as a little of it would have gone a longer way to feed her family.

4 pieces *chye poh*, minced
  or ¼ cup minced *chye poh*
   (preserved radish)
4 eggs
Dash of ground white
  pepper
1½ tablespoons oil

Put the *chye poh* into a sieve and wash it under running water, giving the *chye poh* a few squeezes to get rid of some of the saltiness. Break the eggs into a bowl. Add the minced *chye poh* and the pepper. Beat well to mix the chye poh evenly into the eggs.

Heat one tablespoon of the oil in a non-stick frying pan. Add the egg mixture and fry over medium-high heat. Lift the edge of the omelette with your wok fryer to check the colouring on the underside. If it is a lovely golden brown, turn the omelette over. It doesn't matter that in doing so, you break up the omelette.

Add the remaining half-tablespoon oil around the omelette; lift the edge of the omelette at two or three points and tilt the pan so that the oil can flow beneath the omelette. Allow this side of the omelette to fry till it is golden brown. Turn off the flame. You can cut up the omelette roughly into smaller pieces using the wok fryer or transfer the omelette onto a serving plate and cut it into neat triangular wedges.

Braised Tauhu

In the past, some traditional Teochew families observed a rite of passage ceremony called *chuh huair hnng* (literally, going out to the garden). This event occurred when their children turned fifteen, an age which marked the beginning of adulthood. To commemorate this rite of passage, this special dish of soft soya bean cake was served amongst a variety of other dishes. My family did not observe this ritual, so Mama didn't need to wait until we came of age before she cooked this dish. She cooked it any time she felt like it and because we enjoyed eating it.

1 piece *tauhu*
  (soft soya bean cake)
Oil for frying
2 slices ginger,
  cut into strips
1 clove garlic, minced
½ cup water
4 teaspoons sugar
2 teaspoons light soy sauce
  or fish sauce
1 stalk Chinese celery, cut
  into 2 cm lengths
1 stalk spring onions, cut
  into 2 cm lengths

Blot the *tauhu* gently with kitchen towels to remove excess moisture. Cut it into quarters. Pour oil into a non-stick wok up to a depth of 1 cm. Heat the oil, and then fry the pieces of soya bean cake on both sides until they turn golden. Only turn them over when you see that the lower edges have browned. You may end up breaking them if you are impatient. Once the *tauhu* is fried, transfer them onto kitchen towels to drain away any excess oil.

Reheat the wok with two teaspoons of oil and sauté the ginger strips and minced garlic until they turn golden brown. Add the water, sugar and soy sauce. Stir to dissolve the sugar. Add the pieces of *tauhu* and let them braise in the sweet gravy for about five seconds on each side. Finally, add the Chinese celery and spring onions. Stir gently so as not to break the *tauhu*. Once the greens wilt, which should only take a few seconds, turn off the flame. Transfer to a serving dish.

Glutinous Rice Balls

Once a year, near to the Chinese New Year, when Hua Mama had finished grinding all the rice grains to make her cakes, she would continue to grind glutinous rice that she had first washed and soaked. She sieved the ground glutinous rice to drain it of water to obtain a white, malleable and sticky dough for making glutinous rice balls. Hua Mama sold most of the dough but gave some to Ah Mm, Ah Gou and Mama so they could make their own glutinous rice balls.

The glutinous rice balls that Hua Mama made were nothing like those you find in the frozen section of the supermarket today. The rice balls of my childhood were the size of small marbles, without red bean or black sesame seed paste filling. We ate these rice balls on the seventh day of the Chinese Lunar New Year, a day that was believed to be the universal birthday of mankind. Mama even told us that the number of glutinous rice balls we ate had to correspond with our age. Of course, we did that only with the first serving; after that we ate as many as we wanted. My sisters and I looked forward to the day every year when we got to help Mama roll these little rice balls. Mama would knead red food colouring into one portion of the rice dough so we could make rice balls of two different colours. However, she was always careful about how much red colouring she'd use because she believed that too much food colouring was not good for us. So, we usually ended up with pink or, at the very most, bright gaudy pink rice balls whereas Ah Mm tended to make hers shocking red, much to our amazement and delight.

Today, I think very few people make these glutinous rice balls at home, let alone use a granite millstone to grind rice. For this recipe, I have used glutinous rice flour, so no hard labour is required. Have fun making them!

1 cup glutinous rice flour
½ cup castor sugar or
   brown sugar
4 pandan leaves, tied in a
   knot
2 drops red food colouring
Water

Put 4 cups of water, the sugar and the pandan leaves into a pot and bring to a boil. Let the sugary soup simmer covered for 10 minutes to infuse it with the fragrance of the pandan leaves. If you are using brown sugar, make sure you pack the sugar tightly when you are measuring it. Once the soupy syrup is done, turn off the flame and set it aside. You can reheat it just before serving.

To make the dough, mix the glutinous rice flour and ½ cup of water together in a bowl using your hand. Knead well to make a smooth dough. Remove half of the dough to another bowl and add the red food colouring to it. Knead till the dough is evenly coloured. Making the rice balls is kid's play: just pinch about a teaspoonful of dough and roll it between the palms of your hands to form a little marble. Make as many as you can with both the red and white dough.

While you are making the balls, set another pot of water to boil. When the water is boiling, pop in batches of the rice balls to cook them. When they float, allow a few more seconds of cooking before transferring them with a slotted spoon to the soupy syrup in the other pot. Cook the remaining rice balls in batches and put them in the soup.

You can reheat the soupy syrup with all the rice balls in it if you like to serve it really hot. Otherwise, simply ladle the rice balls together with the soupy syrup into bowls and enjoy.

Poong Kueh

GLUTINOUS RICE CAKE   Makes 16

My first few clumsy attempts at making Poong Kueh caused me to gain a new level of regard for Hua Mama. She single-handedly made hundreds of these *kueh* daily, handling every part of the process herself. She did everything almost like clockwork, having settled into a comfortable rhythm born out of many years of making *kueh*. I will never forget the sight of her sitting on her low wooden stool in her hot, little kitchen with a huge mound of bright pink dough, her hands persistently shaping, wrapping and pinching.

An experienced and instinctive cook, Hua Mama did not measure ingredients but simply estimated the quantities. Thus, Ah Gou, who provided me with this recipe, could not give me exact amounts or proportions. I had to experiment with different combinations of rice flour, tapioca flour and water.

Find your own tempo for making these *kueh*. They will become easier to make as you fine-tune your execution in each step of the process. Don't forget that you will also need a Poong Kueh mould, which you can purchase very inexpensively from bakery supply shops in Chinatown.

FOR THE FILLING

2 cups glutinous rice
4 dried shitake mushrooms
¼ cup dried shrimps
4 cloves garlic
1 tablespoon minced
  chye poh (preserved
  radish)
2 tablespoons oil
1½ teaspoons salt
½ teaspoon monosodium
  glutamate
¼ teaspoon ground white
  pepper
2 tablespoons roasted
  skinless peanuts
2 tablespoons fried shallots
2 cups water

FOR THE DOUGH

1 cup water
4 drops red food
  colouring
1 cup rice flour
1 tablespoon tapioca flour
Extra rice flour for dusting

DIPPING SAUCE

Sweet soya sauce
Chilli sauce

Prepare the filling first by rinsing the shitake mushrooms under running water, and then soaking them in water. Next, wash the glutinous rice and leave it to drain in a sieve. Put the dried shrimps in a strainer and wash under running water, then put them on a folded piece of kitchen towel to absorb the excess moisture. Mince the garlic. Put the *chye poh* in a strainer and wash under running water. Squeeze the *chye poh* to rid it of some of that intense saltiness.

Check on the mushrooms now: they should be fully hydrated. Remove them from the water, letting the excess water drip off without squeezing the mushrooms. Slice them thinly; I find this very efficiently done with a pair of kitchen scissors.

For steaming, I simply convert my wok with a dome-shaped cover into a steamer by placing a metal rack in the centre of the wok. Fill the wok with water up to the level of the rack; cover it and boil the water over a low flame. Oil a cake tin to steam the glutinous rice in.

Cook the filling. Heat 2 tablespoons of oil in a non-stick wok; sauté the sliced mushrooms over a hot fire till they turn deep golden brown. Remove the mushrooms and add the dried shrimps to the remaining oil. Lower the flame and let the dried shrimps fry for about 4 minutes, stirring occasionally till they are crispy. The oil should be bubbling constantly as you fry. If the dried shrimp starts to pop out of the wok, lower the flame slightly but maintain the boiling. Add the minced garlic and *chye poh* when the dried shrimps are almost crispy and continue to fry till the garlic turns golden.

At this point, increase the fire; add the drained glutinous rice, mushrooms, salt, monosodium glutamate and pepper. Stir the mixture for about 10 seconds to coat each grain of rice with the oil and seasonings. Lower the flame and add the water, stirring continuously till the rice absorbs most of the water; this should take about half a minute. Transfer the rice to the oiled caked tin and place it in the wok. Steam over high heat for 30 minutes. Check every 10 or 15 minutes to top up the water in the wok if necessary.

When the rice is ready, mix in the fried peanuts and fried shallots. Cover the steamed glutinous rice with cling foil to prevent it from drying out. Leave the rice to cool slightly while you get on with making the dough.

It is crucial to organize and lay out everything that you require to shape and steam the *kueh* before you begin on the dough. This way, you won't feel harried and stressed when what you need isn't at hand. You have to get ready:

- a pastry brush and a bowl filled with a quarter cup of oil
- a plastic pastry sheet for rolling out the dough
- a rolling pin
- a *poong kueh* mound
- extra rice flour for dusting
- 2 round cake tins to steam the *kueh* in
- 2 round oiled pieces of non-stick baking paper to line the cake tins
- a plate to contain the shaped *kueh*
- an oiled serving plate to serve the steamed *kueh* in
- an oiled spatula for transferring the steamed *kueh*
- a wok with a metal rack and cover for steaming the *kueh*
- a container of water to top up the wok

Once you have all these items ready, you can start making the dough. Heat the water together with the red food colouring in a non-stick pot. Mix the rice flour and tapioca flour in a mixing bowl. Add 1 cup of the boiled coloured water to the flour mixture, stirring continuously. The flour will absorb the water rather quickly to form a crumbly dough. Continue to stir and press the dough for a few more seconds. You will see that some parts of the dough will turn just a little translucent while other parts will still be the original opaque white of the flours. It doesn't matter. Switch to kneading with your hands as soon as you can handle the dough comfortably. Knead till the dough is smooth.

Divide the dough into 16 equal parts. Take one portion of dough, shape it into a circle, coat it all over with rice flour and roll out to a roughly circular shape of about 14 cm diameter. Add a light dusting of rice flour if the dough starts to stick to the pastry sheet or the rolling pin. Hold the rolled dough in your hand, place 2 heaped tablespoons of glutinous rice on the dough; gather the edges of the dough to enclose the filling; press the edges tightly together (it should now look like a Char Siew Bao – Pork Bun), then pinch off the extra dough from the top.

Place this filled dough into the Poong Kueh mould and press gently, flattening and easing it to fill the mould. Turn the mould over and knock it hard against the worktop so that the *kueh* falls out. Place the *kueh* on the oiled non-stick paper in the baking tin. Make enough cakes to fill the tin, leaving a little space between each one. Continue to make cakes with all the glutinous rice. Fill the second baking tin with cakes and leave the remaining ones on the pastry sheet or another plate.

Now prepare the wok as a steamer, placing a metal rack in the centre of the wok and filling the wok with water up to the level of the rack. Cover the steamer and bring the water to a boil. When lots of steam starts to escape from the wok, steam the first batch of Poong Kueh for 10 minutes. Once the first lot is done, remove it from the wok and place the second batch in to steam. Immediately brush the steamed Poong Kueh with oil and let them cool for about 5 minutes or more before transferring them with the oiled spatula to the serving plate. Repeat until all the *kueh* are steamed. Remember to check the water level in the wok and top up when neccessary.

Poong Kueh should be eaten hot. They are traditionally served with sweet soya sauce and chilli sauce.

TIP: The glutinous rice filling can be made a day before and kept in the fridge.

Chinchalok & Lime

BRINED BABY SHRIMP AND LIME

If necessity is the mother of invention, then I think resourcefulness is the result of poverty. It is amazing that people could make something delicious out of the tiniest baby shrimp. These days, very few people eat *chinchalok* the way it was eaten during Hua Mama's days: simply tossed with chillies, thinly sliced shallots and calamansi lime juice then eaten with porridge. Mama still enjoys eating this today. She also uses *chinchalok* as an ingredient to make *kim chi*!

For the best result, *chinchalok* has to be made with the freshest shrimp available. Ah Gou made *chinchalok* all those years ago with baby shrimp that she and Hua Mama caught from the sea. The shrimp were washed in seawater, taken home, and then mixed with a substantial amount of salt to cure them. How much fresher could it get? The shrimp were cured for about a week until they took on a pink hue. Ah Gou then bottled the *chinchalok* for sale. I wanted to try making *chinchalok* but every fishmonger I asked didn't sell these tiny baby shrimp. However, you can get bottled *chinchalok* from the supermarket. As *chinchalok* is so intensely salty, you don't need a whole lot of it as a side dish. The amount specified in this recipe is more than enough for one serving to be eaten with porridge or rice.

2 tablespoons *chinchalok* (brined baby shrimp)
1 *chilli padi* (bird's eye chilli), de-seeded
1 shallot, skinned
2 calamansi limes

Thinly slice the shallot and *chilli padi*. Put the *chinchalok*, shallot and chilli in a small dish; squeeze the juice of the limes over and mix with a pair of chopsticks. That's it.

Soon Kueh

TURNIP DUMPLING   Makes 16

This *kueh* takes a bit of effort to make as the turnip has to be cut into thin strips. However, I rather enjoy this part of the preparation; with a sharp knife, cutting ingredients is a pleasure rather than a pain.

FOR THE FILLING

1 turnip (about 1.1 kg,
    2.4 lbs)
4 dried shitake mushrooms
¼ cup dried shrimps
4 cloves of garlic
2 tablespoons oil
1¾ teaspoons salt
½ teaspoon monosodium
    glutamate
¼ teaspoon of ground
    white pepper
2 cups water
1 teaspoon sugar

FOR THE DOUGH

1 cup water
1 cup rice flour
1 tablespoon tapioca flour
Extra rice flour for dusting

DIPPING SAUCE

Sweet soya sauce
Chilli sauce

Rinse the dried mushrooms under running water and then soak them in a bowl of water. Wash the dried shrimps under running water and put them on a folded piece of kitchen towel to absorb the excess water.

Peel the turnip and wash it well. After peeling the skin, you should be left with about 1 kg of turnip. Cut the turnip into thin slices about 2-3 mm thick. Put about 10 slices of turnip in a stack and cut them into thin strips of about 2-3 mm thick and 2-3 cm long. Continue this way until the whole turnip is cut into strips.

Remove the mushrooms from the water and thinly slice them. Mince the garlic. Heat the oil in a non-stick wok and sauté the mushrooms over high heat till they turn deep golden brown. Remove the mushrooms. Put the dried shrimps in the remaining oil and fry over a medium flame, stirring occasionally, for about 5 minutes. At about the fourth minute, add the garlic. Sauté together with the dried shrimps till the garlic turn golden. Add the turnip strips, mushrooms, salt, monosodium glutamate, sugar and pepper. Stir well to mix the turnip with the other ingredients for the filling. Add the 2 cups of water and stir again. Cover the wok; let the contents simmer for about 20 minutes, stirring every now and then till the turnip is tender. If the water evaporates too quickly, add a bit more so that the turnip can simmer without drying up.

At the end of the 20 minutes, taste to make sure that the turnip is cooked through and tender. If there is too much gravy at this point, remove the cover, increase the heat, and stir till the gravy evaporates. You want a moist filling, not a soggy one. Taste to check if the seasoning is to your taste: add more salt, sugar or pepper if necessary. Transfer the turnip to a big bowl and let it cool slightly while you get on with the rest of the preparation.

Prepare all the things for shaping and steaming the *kueh* before you start on the dough. These are the items you must get ready:

- a pastry brush and a bowl filled with a quarter cup of oil
- a plastic pastry sheet for rolling out the dough
- a rolling pin
- a pair of kitchen scissors to trim the dough
- a bowl with some water to moisten the dough
- extra rice flour for dusting
- 2 round cake tins to steam the *kueh* in
- 2 round oiled pieces of non-stick baking paper to line the cake tins

- a plate to contain the shaped *kueh*
- an oiled serving platter to serve the steamed *kueh* in
- an oiled spatula for transferring the steamed *kueh*
- a wok with a metal rack and cover for steaming the *kueh*
- a container of water to top up the wok

Heat the cup of water in a non-stick pot. Mix the rice flour and tapioca flour in a mixing bowl. Add the boiled water to the flour mixture, stirring continuously. The flour will absorb the water rather quickly to form a crumbly dough. Continue to stir and press the dough for a few more seconds. You will see that some parts of the dough will turn just a little translucent while other parts will still be the original opaque white of the flours. It doesn't matter. Switch to kneading with your hands as soon as you can handle the dough comfortably. Knead till the dough is smooth.

Divide the dough into 16 portions. To shape the Soon Kueh, roll out one portion of dough into a circle of about 10-11 cm in diameter. Hold the round piece of dough in your hand and spoon 2 heaped tablespoons of turnip filling onto the dough.

To seal the dough, you must be somewhat methodical: Dip your ring finger into the bowl of water and moisten half of the edge of the dough. Fold the dough over the filling. Dip your thumb and index finger into the rice flour to coat them well with flour and then press the edges firmly together. (Don't try to seal the *kueh* with wet fingers as the dough will stick to your fingers.) Use kitchen scissors to trim off any excess or untidy edges.

Place the Soon Kueh on the oiled baking paper in the baking tin. Make enough *kueh* to fill the tin. Continue to shape all the *kueh*, filling the second baking tin and leave all the extra ones aside to be steamed later.

Place a metal rack in the centre of the wok and fill the wok with water up to the level of the rack. Cover the wok and bring the water to a boil. When lots of steam starts escaping, steam the *kueh*, one tin at a time for 10 minutes on high heat. Once the *kueh* are steamed, remove from the wok and brush them with oil. Let them cool in the tin for about 5 minutes before transferring them to the serving plate with the oiled spatula. Remember to check the water level in the wok and top up when neccessary.

Serve Soon Kueh with sweet soya sauce and chilli sauce.

Koo Chye Kueh

CHIVE DUMPLING   Makes 16

Koo Chye Kueh is hard to find these days as most hawker stalls only sell Poong Kueh and Soon Kueh. To make Koo Chye Kueh, you need *kee* water. It is alkaline water that softens and lubricates the chives. You can buy *kee* from the dry goods stall at the wet market. It comes as a white or yellow–brown rock. Get the white one; the yellow *kee* is used for making Kee Chang (*kee* rice dumpling). You just need to soak the *kee* in some water and it will slowly dissolve. The *kee* water is clear but feels very slimy. You can remove the *kee*, let it dry and keep it for future use.

FOR THE FILLING
500 g chives
1 tablespoon *kee* water
   (alkaline water)
2 tablespoons lard
1 teaspoon salt
½ teaspoon monosodium
   glutamate

FOR THE DOUGH
1 cup water
1 cup rice flour
1 tablespoon tapioca flour
Extra rice flour for dusting

Trim off any brown ends and yellow tips from the chives. Cut the chives into halves or thirds so they are shorter and easier to wash. Fill a big pot with water and wash the chives well, removing any withered leaves. Rinse twice with fresh water. Shake off as much water as possible and spread out the chives in a colander and blot dry with plenty of kitchen towels. It is very important for the chives to be dry as they will give out a bit of moisture once salt is added. If the chives are wet, there will be too much moisture, which may break the skin of the *kueh*. Once the chives are well dried, cut them into 1 cm lengths. Set aside.

Put the *kee* in a cup and add 2 tablespoons of water to it. Let it soak for 15 minutes till the liquid becomes slimy, then remove the kee. Dry the *kee* and keep for future use. Reserve the *kee* water.

Get the following items ready:

- a pastry brush and a bowl filled with a quarter cup of oil
- a plastic pastry sheet for rolling out the dough
- a rolling pin
- a pair of kitchen scissors to trim the dough
- a bowl with some water to moisten the dough
- extra rice flour for dusting
- 2 round cake tins to steam the *kueh* in
- 2 round oiled pieces of non-stick baking paper to line the cake tins
- a plate to contain the shaped *kueh*
- an oiled serving platter to serve the steamed *kueh* in
- an oiled spatula for transferring the steamed *kueh*,
- a wok with a metal rack and cover for steaming the *kueh*
- a container of water to top up the wok

Proceed to make the dough following the Soon Kueh recipe (see page 38). Divide the dough into 16 parts. Now mix the chives with the lard, *kee* water, salt and monosodium glutamate. Shape and steam the Koo Chye Kueh exactly as you would for Soon Kueh (see page 38). Serve the Koo Chye Kueh with sweet soya sauce and chilli sauce.

Muah Chee

STICKY PEANUT DOUGH

Back when I was a child, we didn't have much in the way of sweet snacks or desserts. The Chinese sweet delicacies we commonly ate were very simple ones. They were usually some sort of sweet soupy dessert like Green Bean Soup, Red Bean Soup, Oh Jut (black rice porridge) or glutinous rice balls in a sweet soupy syrup. Pastries often meant Tau Sah Piah, which was sweet red bean paste or mung bean paste encased in a flaky crust – very delicious, I must say.

Muah Chee happens to be one of Mama's favourite snacks. It is glutinous rice flour and water cooked to a thick yet soft, smooth sticky paste, quite tasteless in itself. Here comes the ingenious part: the glutinous rice paste is flavoured with fried shallots and shallot oil (ingredients we often associate with savoury food), and then cut into small little morsels which are tossed in a mixture of sugar and finely ground roasted peanuts.

Hua Mama sold Muah Chee in the evenings, besides selling glutinous rice ball soup. I can only vaguely remember Hua Mama stirring a huge mass of glutinous rice paste in a black wok. The word "stirring" doesn't even begin to describe the amount of strength she asserted, trying to move that mass around in order to coat it as evenly as possible with the shallot oil. Don't worry, the recipe here makes only a small amount of glutinous rice paste, just enough for you to have fun with. And one more thing – you must eat Muah Chee using toothpicks, a fork or a spoon just won't do!

1 cup glutinous rice flour
1 cup water
1½ cups sugar-coated
  peanuts
¼ cup castor sugar
  (optional)
½ tablespoon shallot oil
1 teaspoon fried shallots
Extra shallot oil

Pound the sugar-coated peanuts finely. Mix the pounded peanuts with the sugar if you like it sweeter (like I do) and set aside on a plate. In a non-stick pot, mix the glutinous rice flour and water together using a spatula until a smooth mixture is obtained.

Heat the pot of glutinous rice liquid over a low fire and stir continuously with the spatula. After a little while of stirring, the liquid will start to cook and thicken. Do not stop stirring, continue until you get a thick paste that does not stick to the bottom or sides of the pot. This paste will stick very stubbornly to your spatula. (If you lift the spatula up, the whole lump of glutinous rice paste will remain stuck to it.) Add the shallot oil and fried shallots to the paste. Stir the dough to coat it with the shallot oil and fried shallots. It is actually more like kneading than stirring! Use an oiled spoon to separate the paste from the spatula so that you can apply the spatula to a different part of the paste and stir more evenly. Keep stirring for about 5 minutes until the glutinous rice paste is uniformly cooked through.

Oil a pair of kitchen scissors with shallot oil and snip off a small piece of the rice paste. Place this on the sugar-peanut mixture to coat it. Cut the remaining paste into small morsels and toss them individually with the sugar and peanut. (Once the paste is coated, they won't stick together.) Transfer them to a serving plate, sprinkle extra sugar-peanut mixture over the Muah Chee and serve immediately, with toothpicks of course!

Shallots, Garlic & Lard

Ah Peh and Ah Mm, whose names are Ng Ee Bak and Soh Ah Siang, stayed just a couple of blocks away from Hua Mama and Ah Gong. So, whenever I visited my grandparents, I would invariably visit Ah Peh and Ah Mm too. We often stayed for dinner at Ah Peh's flat and sampled Ah Mm's cooking.

Ah Peh had been working since he was a little boy on Hua Mama's farm in Kulai. He was responsible for collecting food left over from the pineapple plantation workers' meals and bringing it back to the farm to feed the pigs. When he was a little older, merely ten or eleven years old, Hua Mama would cook a pot of sweet potato soup, then send him off to sell it by the roadside or at the marketplace. I can imagine him as a young child, shabbily dressed, maybe even without shoes, carrying a pot of the soup in one hand and a basket containing ladle, bowls and spoons in the other, calling his wares. Back then, it cost only half-a-cent for a bowl of sweet potato soup; Ah Peh would come back to the farm grinning from ear to ear if he made about ten cents. Of course all the money was handed over to Hua Mama for household expenses.

When Ah Peh got married, he made a living frying and selling Char Kway Teow (Fried Rice Noodles) from a roadside stall he set up near where they stayed in Mang Gah Kah. In 1968, when the family moved to the Bendemeer flat, Ah Peh rented a stall at the market to sell his Char Kway Teow during the day. A few years later, he started to sell Prawn Noodle Soup (page 55) at the same stall. In the evenings, he sold another noodle dish – fried Hokkien Mee (page 79).

Ah Peh's Prawn Noodle Soup was one of the best I have eaten. His soup wasn't the usual deep brown broth but a very pleasant light one. Whenever we were at the stall, he would want to fatten us up with bowls of the steaming hot noodle soup. My cousin, Ah Peh's eldest son, taught me that the best way to savour the prawn soup was to get some *you char kway* (fried dough sticks), dunk them in the prawn soup and enjoy!

Ah Mm and Ah Peh's small and cluttered kitchen was filled with the many ingredients used for making Prawn Noodle Soup. One corner was stacked with big packets of *bee hoon* (rice vermicelli) while the fridge was filled with pork bones, large slabs of pork, bags of prawns and bigger bags of yellow noodles. There seemed to be always something being cooked on the stove, whether it was soup, or shallots or the day's meals for the family.

Ah Peh has retired as a hawker. At seventy-seven, he is still quite youthful-looking, tanned and sturdy with a head of fairly black hair. Unlike many men of his age, he doesn't carry around a huge beer belly, just a slight middle-age paunch. He is usually dressed in bermudas and a white singlet. I remember when my sisters and I were younger and visited him at his flat or his Char Kway Teow stall, he would greet us with a wide, hearty smile. He always insisted on frying a plate or two of *kuay teow* for us, sometimes even making his customers wait while he did so. "You must eat," he would chide in mock anger, "You're all so skinny like bamboo poles… your mother doesn't feed you enough… it's just a little bit of *kuay teow* anyway, not even enough to fill the gaps between your teeth!"

Ah Mm, on the other hand, is plump, with naturally wavy hair cut short because she is not one to fuss with her appearance. She just makes sure to clip any loose strands of hair well away from her face. Even the blouse and pants of the samfu that she wears daily are mismatched. She is the ultimate homebody. Other than making trips to the wet market, she has no interest in going anywhere else, except perhaps to visit Mama or

Ah Gou when an occasion calls for it.

To me, Ah Mm is the primary support system behind the scene to three generations of hawkers in her family: her mother-in-law, husband and children. From the time when Hua Mama started selling a variety of *kueh* at Mang Gah Kah, Ah Mm had to help prepare the glutinous rice, chives and turnip fillings for these *kueh*. She woke up at three in the morning to start the charcoal fire. Then there were turnips to be peeled, cut and then fried; this was the filling for the Soon Kueh. She had to mince huge amounts of garlic, shell cockles and prawns, fry the sliced shallots, as well as cook the lard and prepare the chilli paste for Ah Peh's Char Kway Teow and Prawn Noodle Soup businesses. Later, when Hua Mama and Ah Mm's third son operated a Kway Chap stall at the Bendemeer market, Ah Mm was the one who again prepared the fried shallots and made the special chilli sauce. Everything was prepared by hand from scratch.

Whenever we visited Ah Mm, we would find her sitting on a low wooden stool on the floor, busily peeling and slicing a big basket of onions and garlic. I always marvelled that she did not shed a single tear when she dealt with those onions. I remember evenings spent with my cousin separating the layers of *kway chap*. It was absolutely non-essential work as the layers of *kway chap* would come apart once they were blanched in water. But we had a good time holding a thick stack of very oily rice sheets and carefully separating them just for the fun of it.

Ah Mm's little flat was perpetually filled with

this distinctive amalgamation of smells of fried lard, peeled onions, garlic, fried chilli paste and other food she was in the process of preparing. I will never forget that huge wok of lard frying on the stove, so fragrant yet a bit cloying at the same time. The lard was needed not just for Ah Peh's Char Kway Teow but also for their family meals, so Ah Mm had to prepare batches very frequently. She fried shallots every other day, and ground and cooked the chilli paste once a week. She took all these chores in her stride daily, on top of cooking three meals, cleaning and hand washing the laundry for all the ten people in her family, including my grandparents. Later, when Ah Peh sold Prawn Noodle Soup, Ah Mm had to cook huge quantities of prawns and peel them. She seemed to be continually doing one chore after another. For her, having a cup of coffee in the afternoon while slicing onions or peeling prawns amounted to a break.

When I stayed with Hua Mama and Ah Gong during my first year of schooling, I had dinner at Ah Mm's place from Monday to Friday. Her cooking was homey and rustic; she was very generous with the lard which imparted moisture and smoothness to the food. She unapologetically used monosodium glutamate to enhance flavours. It was understandable because, being poor, she couldn't spare the expense of making good stock to give flavour to her cooking.

I absolutely loved the fish that Ah Mm fried and then braised with dark soy sauce, ginger and garlic. Her fried cauliflower with green bell pepper was tender and oily – sinful but good. Ah Mm also learned to cook curry chicken (page 52).

I call it "Chinese curry" as it is not as complex as Malay or Thai curries with their many layers of flavours. Hers was delicious in its simplicity – an unforgettable taste of my childhood. Although she diligently cooked the meals for her family, she had very simple tastes, preferring a humble bowl of plain porridge with a bit of preserved bean curd or a wedge of salted egg.

On Hua Mama and Ah Gong's birthdays, Ah Mm made Sweet Birthday Noodles that we ate with hard-boiled or soft-boiled eggs (page 47). The long strands of noodles represented the long life we wished upon our grandparents and the sweet soup symbolized a sweet, happy existence. It was a dish I looked forward to having every year.

Ah Mm's front door was never closed. Her children's friends could come and go at any time, have meals in her kitchen, and even sleep over.

Virtually untouched by the changes in the twenty-first century, she wears the same type of *samfu* (pantsuit) as yesteryear. She is not seduced by the trappings of wealth. She is not even tempted to have a meal at a restaurant and practically had to be arm-twisted to attend her children's wedding dinners. Perhaps it is her shyness or a lifetime of hardship that had robbed her of the ability to enjoy the finer things in life.

As I think about my childhood, especially the year I lived with my grandparents and ate so many meals cooked by Ah Mm, I am filled with warm memories of the simple, yet delicious, food we enjoyed as a family.

Sweet Birthday Noodles

serves 4

These days, we celebrate birthdays with cream cakes, candles and presents. No one remembers to cook these sweet noodles anymore. The notion of sweet noodles may be confounding but you must try them before passing judgement. I always ate the noodles and the egg white first, leaving the best part, the yolk, for later. I would pop the entire yolk into my mouth and let the creamy yolk run all over, savouring it for as long as I could before swallowing. Divine! Finally, I washed everything down with the sweet broth, a fitting end to a delightful treat. Occasionally, I would break and stir the yolk into the broth and drink the eggy soup to the very last drop. I am definitely going to cook these sweet noodles on my children's birthdays from now on.

3 bundles, about 200 g
   mee kia (fine egg noodles)
6 cups water
¾ cup sugar
4 pandan leaves, knotted
4 eggs

Boil the water, sugar and pandan leaves in a pot to make the soup. Let it simmer for 5 minutes. Set another pot of water to boil. Loosen each bundle of *mee kia* so the strands won't stick when you cook them later. Divide the noodles into 4 portions. When the water boils, put one portion of *mee kia* into the boiling water, stirring with a pair of chopsticks to separate the strands. Let the water come back to a boil and cook the noodles for about 10 more seconds, lowering the flame if the water is bubbling too vigorously. Drain the noodles and put them into a bowl. Cook the other portions of noodles in the same way. Just before you cook the last portion of noodles, start reheating the sweet broth.

Break an egg into each bowl of noodles then ladle the hot bubbling soup onto the noodles but not directly onto the yolks. They may break if you do so. Stir the whites into the hot soup so the heat of the broth gently cooks them. The yolks will remain fairly liquid. Let the noodles soak in the soup to absorb some of its sweetness.

If you prefer hardboiled eggs, cook these before you start on the soup and noodles. With enough water, completely immerse the 4 eggs in a pot. I tend to do this with cold eggs straight from the fridge. When the water comes to a boil, lower the flame and cook for a further 5 minutes. Remove the eggs and shell them after they have cooled. For birthdays, the hardboiled eggs are traditionally dyed with red food colouring before shelling.

Tang Hoon Soup

MUNG BEAN VERMICELLI SOUP

serves 4

Ah Mm cooked this Tang Hoon Soup quite frequently during the year I stayed with my grandparents. Sometimes, I had this soup on its own as it had everything that is needed for a healthy and balanced meal: protein, carbohydrates and vegetables. I remember the first time my son ate *tang hoon*, he called it "virtual noodles" on account of how transparent the *tang hoon* was. The smooth and slippery texture of the *tang hoon* was quite a surprise to him as it was so different from other kinds of noodles. Yet that is what makes *tang hoon* so fun to eat. So slurp away!

2 cups of split boneless
  ikan bilis (whitebait)
6 cups water
80 g *tang hoon*
  (mung bean vermicelli)
1½ tablespoon *tang chye*
  (preserved vegetables)
1 stalk Chinese celery
1 stalk spring onion
1 bunch Chinese lettuce
20 fresh fishballs
1 red chilli or 2 *chilli padi*
  (bird's eye chilli)
Light soy sauce
Ground white pepper
Shallot oil
Fried shallots

Start by making the *ikan bilis* stock. Put the *ikan bilis* in a big strainer and wash under running water. Drain the excess water and put the *ikan bilis* in a pot. Add 6 cups of water then bring it to a boil. Lower the flame and cover the pot tightly. Simmer it over a low fire for 30 minutes and make sure to add more water to replace what has evaporated during the simmering process.

Soak the *tang hoon* in water and go on to prepare the other ingredients. Put the *tang chye* in a strainer, rinse it under running water and set aside. Chop the Chinese celery, dice the spring onions and set them aside. Separate the leaves of the Chinese lettuce and wash each leaf under running water. Shake off the excess water and put the leaves in a colander to dry.

Bring another small pot of water to a boil and cook half the *tang hoon* for about a minute. Drain the excess water and divide the *tang hoon* into 2 bowls. Repeat with the remaining *tang hoon*.

When the *ikan bilis* stock is done, strain the soup into another pot and discard the *ikan bilis*. Turn on the flame and bring the soup to a simmer. Add the fishballs to the soup and let them cook gently until they float. Simmer for two more minutes before turning off the flame. Taste the soup and add salt to your taste. Cover the soup to keep it warm.

Thinly slice the red chilli and divide the slices among 4 small dipping dishes; add light soy sauce to each dish. Ladle the hot soup and fishballs over the *tang hoon* in each bowl. Garnish the dish with the *tang chye*, Chinese lettuce, Chinese celery, spring onions, pepper, shallot oil and fried shallots. Serve with the dishes of sliced chilli.

Dried Shrimp Noodles

serves 4

I love this dish for its unusual but flavoursome soup, its short cooking time, and the dried shrimps that retain much of their flavour. Use three bundles of noodles to prepare four servings as the *mee kia* tends to swell after absorbing some of the soup stock. A word of caution about cucumbers: I always buy one more cucumber than I need because every now and then I will come across an inedible bitter cucumber. Cut a thin slice from each end of the cucumber and taste. Discard the cucumber if it's at all bitter. A better solution would be to get Japanese cucumbers.

½ cup dried shrimps,
  washed and drained
1 large cucumber, peeled
1 tablespoon oil
2 cloves garlic,
  finely minced
2 cups canned chicken
  stock
4 cups water
¾ teaspoon salt
3 bundles, about 200 g
  mee kia (fine egg noodles)
Ground white pepper

Cut the cucumber into quarters, lengthwise, cutting away the seeds. Slice each strip of cucumber diagonally into pieces about ½ centimetre thick. Heat the oil in a big pot then sauté the dried shrimps over low heat till you can see lots of foaming. If the shrimps start popping out of the pot, lower the flame. Fry the shrimps for about 5 minutes or until you can detect a change in the fragrance to a very slight burnt smell. This smell doesn't mean the dried shrimps are burnt, just that they are well fried and crisp. Add the garlic and continue to sauté until the garlic turns golden brown. Include the cucumber and stir well. Pour in the chicken broth, water and add the salt. Let the soup come to a boil, then simmer it covered for 8 to 10 minutes. The cucumber slices will soften quite quickly.

Meanwhile, boil another pot of water to cook the *mee kia*. Divide the noodles into four portions. Remember to loosen the noodles so that the strands don't stick together when they are cooking. When the water boils, put one portion of *mee kia* into the boiling water, stirring with a pair of chopsticks to separate the strands. Let the water come back to a boil and cook the noodles for about 10 more seconds, lowering the flame if the water boils too vigorously. Drain the noodles and put them into a bowl. Cook the other portions of noodles in the same way.

Ladle the soup over the noodles, top with some cucumber, dried shrimps and pepper.

Ah Mm's Curry Chicken

serves 6-8

This is the curry chicken of my childhood: it is a mellow orange with red flecks of chilli. Ah Mm cooked this curry on almost all the festive occasions when we visited. As it was never too spicy, I enjoyed drinking the curry like a soup.

The coconut milk that Ah Mm used was extracted from the flesh of a freshly grated coconut as canned or packaged coconut milk wasn't available to her then. The coconut milk from the first pressing was thick and creamy and was added to the curry at the end of the cooking process. This is because the milk should not be boiled or the oil will separate and you won't get that creamy consistency in the curry gravy. After the first pressing, Ah Mm added water to the grated coconut and squeezed out as much residual milk as possible. This second pressing of coconut milk was much thinner than the first. It was added to the curry to provide the liquid for braising the chicken in. I use regular chillies in this recipe, but if you like it really hot then substitute with an equal number of *chilli padi* (birds' eye chilli).

Eat this curry with French loaf, boiled rice or *bee hoon* (rice vermicelli) simply fried with garlic and bean sprouts. Just dip the bread into the curry or ladle a generous amount of the curry over the rice or *bee hoon* and enjoy!

1 chicken (about 1 kg)
2 stalks lemongrass
2 large potatoes
20 shallots
6 cloves garlic
8 red chillies, deseeded
6 candlenuts
2 thumb-size pieces
    turmeric
1 thumb-size piece galangal
1 tablespoon *belacan*
    (shrimp paste)
2 cups water
5 tablespoons oil
1¼ teaspoons salt
250 g packet coconut milk

Cut the chicken into serving pieces; you should have about 17 to 20 pieces in all. Remove the skin if you like. Get rid of the bishop's nose and set the cut chicken aside. Remove the outer leaves of the lemongrass if they are brown. Cut each stalk into 2 or 3 pieces and smash each piece. Peel the potatoes and cut each one into bite-size pieces. Soak the pieces of potato in water to prevent them from turning brown.

To pound the curry paste ingredients using the mortar and pestle, roughly chop up the shallots, garlic, chilli, candlenuts, turmeric, galangal and *belacan* before pounding. This will make it easier for you to pound and greatly reduce the time required to do so.

To grind the ingredients in a blender, put the shallots, garlic, chilli, candlenuts, turmeric, galangal and *belacan* into the blender. Add the 5 tablespoons of oil to the ingredients. Use the pulse function to have better control and avoid grinding everything too smoothly.

To cook the curry, heat the 5 tablespoons oil in a non-stick wok and fry the pounded curry paste. For the blended paste mixture, there is no need to add any oil to the wok as the oil has been blended together with the paste ingredients. Fry the curry paste over medium to medium-high heat for 5 to 8 minutes till fragrant and the oil separates. Add the chicken pieces and stir to coat them with the paste. Add the water as well as the salt and potatoes. Bring to a gentle boil, cover and simmer for 15 minutes.

Remove the pieces of breast meat to a bowl as they tend to cook and dry out faster. Cover the wok again and continue to simmer for another 15 to 20 minutes until the red meat of the chicken and potatoes are tender. Return the pieces of breast meat to the wok and add the coconut milk. There is no need to increase the flame. Just stir gently until the curry is heated through. Turn off the flame. Taste to check if it is salted to your taste and adjust accordingly.

Prawn Noodle Soup

serves 4

A home-cooked version of Prawn Noodle Soup can easily be produced to rival the version of a seasoned hawker. I use pork ribs instead of lean pork as my husband loves his Prawn Noodle Soup with ribs. The prawn soup for Ah Peh's recipe is light coloured. Ah Peh's secret to making it taste heavenly is sugar and a touch of monosodium glutamate. It's that simple.

400 g pork bones

400 g pork ribs

400g medium prawns, unshelled

6 cups water

2½ teaspoons salt

1 tablespoon sugar

¼ teaspoon monosodium glutamate

8 large cloves garlic, smashed

300 g fresh yellow noodles

300 g *kuay teow* (flat rice noodles)

2 cups bean sprouts

1 cooked fishcake, sliced

Fried shallots

Shallot oil

Ground white pepper

2 red chillies, thinly sliced

Light soy sauce

Wash the pork bones, pork ribs and prawns. Put the pork bones and ribs in a big pot. Add the water, salt, sugar, monosodium glutamate and smashed garlic. Bring to a boil then lower the flame. Cover the pot and simmer for 5 minutes. Add the prawns to the simmering broth and let them blanch in the gently heated soup until they turn completely opaque and deep orange-red. Remove the prawns and set them aside to cool. Cover the pot and let the broth simmer for 2 hours until the ribs are fall-off-the-bone tender. When the prawns have cooled enough to be handled, shell them. Put all the shells, heads and tails back into the pot to be simmered together with the pork bones and ribs. The prawns can be left whole or sliced lengthwise into half.

After the broth has simmered for 2 hours, add water to make up for that lost to evaporation. Bring the broth back to a boil. Remove the pieces of pork ribs and set them aside. Strain the broth through a sieve into another pot. Taste and adjust the seasoning if needed. Remember that the broth has to taste slightly saltier than you wish as the taste will balance out when you have added the noodles, *kuay teow* and bean sprouts. Return the pork ribs to the soup. You can cook this soup in advance, even a day before; then simply let it cool and store it in the fridge. The cooked prawns and pork should also be refrigerated until needed.

When you are ready to serve, reheat the soup. At the same time, bring another pot of water to the boil. Once the water comes to a rolling boil, throw in all the bean sprouts at once and blanch them for just a couple of seconds so they can remain firm and crunchy. Remove the bean sprouts with a sieve and set them aside. Separate the noodles and *kuay teow* into 4 portions. Let the water come back to a boil. Blanch the noodles one portion at a time for about 10 seconds. Remember you must let the water come back to a boil again before blanching each portion of noodles. Put the blanched noodles directly into each serving bowl.

Top each bowl of noodles with the bean sprouts. Arrange the prawns, pork ribs and fishcake slices attractively on top. Ladle the boiling soup into the bowl; avoid pouring the soup directly onto the prawns if they have been sliced as the hot soup will further cook the prawns causing them to overcook. Add fried shallots, shallot oil and a dash of pepper. Serve immediately with little individual dishes of sliced red chillies and light soy sauce.

Chinese Rice Wine

Ng Bak Eng, my Ah Gou, is my father's older sister. They shared a remarkable resemblance: their eyes and the lines of their jaws were so similar. She is also quite tall, trim and has an amazing figure for a woman who has borne five children.

Ah Gou spent the first eight to nine years of her life on Hua Mama's vegetable farm. Growing up on a farm meant she had to pitch in to help as soon as she was old enough to do so. As was the way in those days, girls, especially those from poor families, were not sent to school. Hua Mama would tell her, "Girls don't need to study; they must learn to do the chores at home. You'll get married later and will belong to your in-laws. So there's no need for you to go to school."

Ah Gou's daily chores included watering the vegetables, picking the ripe chillies and ladies' fingers, digging up the root vegetables and even bathing the pigs. In the house, she had to make the beds, sweep the floor, wash the dishes, and help with the preparation of meals. Her favourite task was to keep a look out for birds that came to steal a bite of the crops. She would sit by a scarecrow my grandfather had placed next to a little stream that flowed by the vegetable plot. A long rope was tied to this scarecrow and empty tin cans were attached to the rope. Every now and then, Ah Gou had to give the rope a tug to rattle the tin cans. The din that resulted would scare away any prospecting birds. That had to be pretty fun for a young girl used to the unchanging and mundane routine of farm life; it was the only leisure she knew.

After all that hard work on the farm, you would think mealtimes afforded an opportunity to relax with the family and enjoy some time away from farm chores. But this was not the case. Ah Gou remembers how strict my grandfather was at the table: he would rap the children on the head with his knuckles if they ate too slowly. "How come you haven't made a dent in your rice?" If they ate too much of the side dishes, that was deserving of a knock on the head as well. They had to eat their meals quickly and quietly.

Ah Gou recalled hearing rumours of the impending Japanese war and learning of neighbours fleeing their farms. As a child, even when she could hear the faint rumblings of bombs exploding in the distance, the war was still unreal to her. There was nothing like newspapers or television images to make the horrors of the war real for her. On 31 January 1942, British troops blew up part of the Causeway to impede the Japanese' advance. Ah Gou heard the thunderous explosions, felt the terrible tremors under her feet, and saw the sky turn crimson red in an instant. She finally realized that war was at her doorstep.

Life in Singapore was just as hard when Ah Gou lived with Hua Mama in the *hai tnoinh choo*. Hua Mama, who drove herself to work harder than anyone would expect of her, made sure that Ah Gou didn't idle any precious time away. When Hua Mama was up and out the house at dawn to sell fish, Ah Gou had to do all the household chores like cooking, cleaning and washing. The charcoal fire for cooking also had to be started way ahead of time. Every day, Ah Gou had to row a sampan to the mainland to collect water from the public tap. She had no time for dilly-dallying as she needed to fetch the water and row back to the house at sea before the tide went down. If there was any free time, she would go to the beach to catch small crab-like creatures called *baa kee*. She washed them in seawater before bringing them home to be cured in salt, garlic and chillies, in much the same way she made *chinchalok* and *gao nee*.

Hua Mama and Ah Gou stayed in the *hai tnoinh choo* for three years. When Hua Mama remarried, they all moved to Mang Gah Kah to live in the house that Ah Gong built. Ah Gou continued to help out at home with all the usual chores. There was even a season when she worked as a domestic maid for fifteen dollars a month. Of course, every cent had to be handed over to Hua Mama.

As was the custom in those days, when Ah Gou was just thirteen or fourteen years old, Hua Mama started getting matchmakers to find a suitable potential husband for her. If a girl was not married by the age of eighteen or nineteen, she was considered an old maid! Poor Ah Gou  was so terrified of the different matchmakers and the prospect of getting married that she ran away to hide in the outhouse whenever a matchmaker came to visit.

Once, a matchmaker arranged for Hua Mama and Ah Gou to meet a potential partner in Gay World. Ah Gou went along, blissfully unaware that the meeting was to discuss the terms of a marriage. Hua Mama had baited Ah Gou with a new dress. Being naïve and innocent, Ah Gou was happy just to be wearing it for an outing. At the meeting, Hua Mama sang praises of her daughter while negotiating for more generous bridal gifts from the prospective groom's family. Hua Mama understandably wanted Ah Gou to marry well. The matchmaker, representing the groom, promised many gifts including pieces of jewellery, clothes and roast pigs. Upon hearing

THIS PAGE: *Gay World Amusement Park.*
FACING PAGE: *Ah Gou's wedding picture. She was just nineteen.*

all this, Hua Mama was only too happy to agree. However, both parties had to wait for three days before meeting again to finalize the match. Within these three days, no crockery should be broken in either of their homes or the match would be off. You see, they believed that such an ominous sign meant that the marriage would end up broken as well. I can only imagine how careful Hua Mama was when handling breakable items and would have warned Ah Gou to exercise the same extreme caution too. But guess what? Hua Mama broke a porcelain soup spoon on the second day! When Hua Mama met up with the matchmaker again, she went without any intention of mentioning the broken spoon. However, the matchmaker had a change of tune. All of a sudden she was making excuses concerning why the prospective groom's family would not be giving as many gifts. Hua Mama was so annoyed that she called off the match, much to Ah Gou's relief.

Ah Gou finally married at the age of nineteen. Her husband, whom I addressed as Ah Tnionh, was not a wealthy man at all. He was an orphan who made very little money selling coffee at a makeshift coffee stand by the roadside. However, Hua Mama was unexpectedly fond of him, probably out of pity at first, as she had lived a hard life herself. Ah Gou put it down to fate and serendipity.

Shortly after their wedding, Ah Tnionh became a bus driver. He lost his job after the Hock Lee bus strike in 1955 and returned to selling coffee to support his family. By then, Ah Gou had given birth to three children, and they had moved several times, living in rented rooms, as they family grew. It was when their fifth child was born that Ah Tnionh got involved in the lumber trade. His business prospered so the family was able to settle down in their own flat and, later on, even buy a house.

It was Ah Tnionh who taught Ah Gou to make Chinese rice wine (page 63). He first made the wine during her confinement month after the birth of their second child. Since then, Ah Gou has been making the wine herself. She is definitely the undisputed expert when it comes to winemaking. Today, she regularly makes this wine for drinking and uses the rice wine residue (*ang zhao*) for cooking (page 65).

From a little girl who had no choice but occupy her place in the kitchen, Ah Gou has developed a passion for cooking today. Now she is happy to go to the wet market every day and cook to her heart's content for her children and grandchildren. She has come a long way from preparing the simple food of so long ago. Now she does restaurant-style steamed fish, sharks fin soup, *teriyaki* kebabs and a variety of other dishes which she never had the opportunity to eat as a child. Nonetheless, she frequently returns to her roots and will cook a meal of her specialties from days gone by for her family to enjoy.

FACING PAGE: (Top left) *Ah Gou, seated right, with her friends;* (top right) *Ah Gou and Hua Mama;* (bottom) *Ah Gou and Ah Tnionh looking fashionable with their new car.*

Chinese Rice Wine

Produces 1 litre of wine and 1½ cups of rice residue

The Chinese have engaged in the domestic production of rice wine for centuries. Inexpensive and easy to produce at home, rice wine is highly regarded for its health-giving properties, especially for women who have just given birth. The rice wine is believed to help her body regain the energy that was expended in childbirth and keep her warm.

As a young girl, I was appalled by the pungent smell of the wine, bewildered that people would actually drink that vile liquid. I was also disconcerted by the *ang zhao* (rice residue), a mushy, mouldy-looking mess in unappetizing shades of red. Mama was given bottles of this homemade wine and jars of the rice residue after she had given birth to my brothers. The wine was usually brought by some aunties or friends when they visited. Their conversations always included a discussion on the length of fermentation of the rice wine, how sweet and *jiak* (warming to the body) the wine was, what a lovely shade of pink/red it was, and the sharing of a couple of recipes using the wine or the wine residue.

The *chiu bianh* (wine cakes), which is a fermenting agent, converts the starch in the rice into sugars, giving the wine its natural sweetness. I buy the wine cakes and *ang kark* (red rice grains) from Chinese medical shops. The red rice grains impart their cranberry red hue to the wine. The amount of red rice added will determine how red the wine will be.

500 g glutinous rice grains
1 piece wine cake
4 cups water
½ cup boiled water at room temperature
3 tablespoons red rice grains

Wash a clay pot or an earthen pot large enough to hold all the ingredients with room to spare. Let the pot dry well overnight. Wash the glutinous rice well. Let it soak in water for about 30 minutes, then drain well. Put the rice into a large microwave-proof pot with the 4 cups of water. Put the lid on but allow a gap for the steam to escape. Microwave on high for 12 minutes. Let the rice rest covered for another 20 minutes so it will continue to cook in the residual heat. In the meantime, pound the wine cake into a white powder. Next pound the red rice grains coarsely. Set both aside.

Uncover the pot of glutinous rice and let it cool completely. Divide the glutinous rice, the pounded wine cake and red grains into three portions each. Put one portion of glutinous rice in an even layer at the bottom of the clay pot. Sprinkle one portion of the red rice grains over the glutinous rice, followed by the pounded wine cake. Lastly, sprinkle one-third of the half cup of water over everything. Repeat these steps with a second layer then use the remaining ingredients for the third and final layer.

Cover the clay pot. Put a double layer of aluminium foil over the top and sides of the pot and trim the corners so that it can fit neatly around the pot. Seal the edges of the foil with two rounds of a broad-width tape, pressing the tape down firmly to ensure that the pot is airtight. The wine will be ready in 30 day's time. Make a note of this and stick it on the pot.

On the 29th day, wash a screw-top glass bottle of 1-litre capacity and a jar. Dry both thoroughly. Finally, on the 30th day, remove the foil from the pot. A sharp alcoholic smell will instantly tell you that you have succeeded in making rice wine. The glutinous rice and red rice grains will form a mushy layer on top of the wine. Scoop the wine out and strain it through a sieve into a large container, leaving behind the rice residue with just a little wine left to keep it moist. Store the rice residue in the jar. With the help of a funnel, transfer the wine into the bottle. Screw on the tops and keep both in the fridge. At this stage, the wine will be murky but the fine residue will settle at the bottom of the bottle, leaving a lovely clear cranberry-red wine.

Ang Zhao Mee Sua

RICE WINE VERMICELLI SOUP
serves 4

This is Ah Gou's famous Rice Wine Vermicelli Soup that she cooks regularly for her family and guests lucky enough to be invited to her home for a meal. The soup is extremely flavoursome with the *ang zhao* (rice wine residue) as well as the addition of Benedictine DOM, which you can substitute with Yomeishu or XO if you like.

4 chicken carcasses
   (with necks)
1 chicken breast
6 cups water
1 tablespoon oil
8 cloves garlic, smashed
8 slices ginger
6 tablespoons *ang zhao*
6 tablespoons *Benedictine*
   DOM
1¼ teaspoons salt
½ tablespoon sugar
2 chicken legs, cut into
   bite-sized pieces
6 bundles, about 180 g
   mee sua (flour vermicelli)
Coriander leaves

Wash the chicken backs, neck and chicken breast. Cut them into smaller pieces. Put the chicken pieces in a pot with the 6 cups of water. Be sure to take note of the water level. Bring the contents to a boil, then cover the pot and let it simmer for 1 hour. At the end of the simmering, add water to bring it to the original water level and then bring the broth back to a boil. Strain the broth through a sieve into another pot and skim off the fat on top. You can prepare this broth a day ahead, strain it and leave it in the fridge. The next day, the fat will solidify in an opaque layer. You can easily remove this layer of fat so the broth is ready for use.

Heat the oil in a pot. Add the garlic and ginger and fry for a while until they start to turn golden and are very fragrant. Add the *ang zhao* and continue to fry for a few more seconds before adding the Benedictine Dom, stirring well to let the wine release its flavour as well as for the alcohol to evaporate. Add all the chicken broth, salt and sugar and bring everything to a boil. When the soup starts to boil, lower the heat and immerse the cut-up chicken legs in it. Let the chicken pieces poach gently in the simmering soup for 15 minutes.

To assemble the dish, bring a pot of water to boil. Divide the *mee sua* into 4 portions, allowing 1½ bundles per portion. Cook the *mee sua*, one portion at a time in the boiling water, stirring with a pair of chopsticks to separate the strands. *Mee sua* cooks very fast, requiring just 1 – 1½ minutes. Drain the *mee sua* and transfer it to a bowl. Cook the other portions of *mee sua* in the same way. Add the soup to the *mee sua* and top with the chicken and coriander leaves.

Steamed White Pomfret

serves 4 - 6

Teochew food has the distinction of having a light, clean and clear taste, letting each ingredient speak for itself yet complimenting one another and combining to make one lovely delectable whole. This characteristic is most clearly exemplified in this dish of steamed white pomfret, which you can find in the menus of Teochew restaurants.

A dish like this undoubtedly calls for the freshest of ingredients; there can be no compromise, especially where the pomfret is concerned. You must steam the fish on the day it is caught.

1 white pomfret
   (about 600 g)
1 cup chicken stock
1 dried shitake mushroom
1 leaf of *kiam chye*
   (salted mustard green)
½ tomato
1 piece pork fat (1 x 3 cm)
6 slices of ginger
2 sour plums
1 stalk spring onion
1 stalk coriander leaves
2 red chillies
Light soy sauce

Wash the fish and clean the stomach cavity thoroughly. Dry the fish with kitchen towels and cut parallel slits on each side of the fish, all the way to the bones. Place the fish on a plate on which it will be steamed in and served. Set this aside. The fish must be at room temperature before steaming.

Rinse the shitake mushroom and soak it in half a bowl of water. Use only the thick, fleshy part of the *kiam chye* leaf. Slice it thinly and place the strips in a big bowl of water. Use your hand to squeeze the *kiam chye* well; this helps to rid it of its intense saltiness quickly. Throw the *kiam chye* water away and repeat the process. Now taste a bit of the *kiam chye* to check if the level of saltiness is to your liking. If it is still too salty, repeat the process and then drain the *kiam chye*. Set aside.

Cut the tomato thinly. Slice the pork fat into very thin slivers. Cut the ginger slices into strips. Remove the mushroom from the water and thinly slice it.

For the garnish, thinly cut the spring onion on the diagonal and cut the coriander leaves into shorter lengths. Cut one chilli in half lengthwise. Remove the seeds and cut each half into long thin strips. Soak the spring onions, coriander leaves and chilli strips in water.

Slice the other chilli and transfer it to a small dipping dish. Add light soy sauce and set this aside to be served with the steamed pomfret.

When you are ready to steam the fish, bring the water in the steamer to the boil. Arrange the tomato slices, the *kiam chye*, mushroom, pork fat and sour plums around the pomfret. Pour the chicken stock and 1 table-spoon of light soy sauce into a small pot.

When steam begins to escape from the steamer, do not open it. Instead, heat up the stock and bring it to a boil. Once it is boiling hot, pour it over the pomfret and place the fish in the steamer. Steam over high heat for 5-6 minutes.

Garnish with the spring onions, coriander leaves and chilli strips. Serve the fish immediately with the dip of sliced chilli and soy sauce.

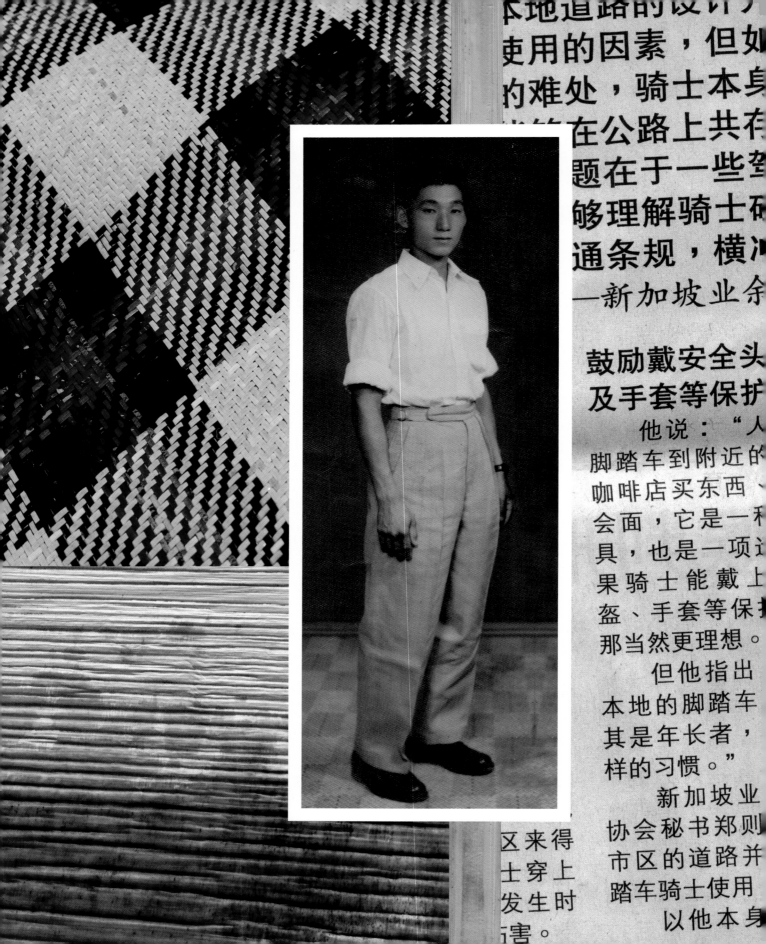

本地道路的设计了
使用的因素，但如
的难处，骑士本身
的在公路上共存
题在于一些驾
够理解骑士砸
通条规，横冲

——新加坡业余

鼓励戴安全头
及手套等保护

他说："人
脚踏车到附近的
咖啡店买东西、
会面，它是一种
具，也是一项运
果骑士能戴上
盔、手套等保护
那当然更理想。

但他指出
本地的脚踏车
其是年长者，
样的习惯。"

新加坡业
协会秘书郑则
市区的道路并
踏车骑士使用

区来得
士穿上
发生时
害。

以他本身

Sin Chew Bee Hoon & Ginger Strings

If Hua Mama had not sent my father ahead to Singapore to live with a relative during the Japanese Occupation, Papa might have become a hawker like Hua Mama. Instead, Ng Kin Bak followed in the footsteps of that relative and became a car mechanic. Regardless, the ability to cook must be something that runs in the family because Papa was a great cook. His fried Hokkien Mee (page 78), Sin Chew Bee Hoon (page 77), Loh Mee (page 87) and stir-fried vegetables (page 73) were some of our all-time favourites. In a way, I believe that not having to depend on cooking to make a living allowed Papa to truly enjoy being in the kitchen.

When I was young, Mama was the one who did the cooking daily; I don't recall Papa cooking anything until I was about seven or eight years old. At that time, he would occasionally fry *bee hoon* and a batch of chicken wings on Sundays. Sometimes, he cooked a pot of chicken curry to be eaten with *bee hoon* simply fried with just bean sprouts and garlic. There was no need for other ingredients in the *bee hoon* as we ladled a

generous amount of curry over it and enjoyed every mouthful. Papa would cook a meal on a whim at any time, even a late-night supper. He would cook his special *bee hoon* with seafood (page 75), or with whatever ingredients he had on hand. We had a fridge by then, signalling the end of Mama's daily trip to the wet market. The fridge was usually well stocked with prawns, fish, pork, eggs and vegetables. I remember helping him wash the *chye sim* while he prepared the other ingredients, then standing by watching as he fried the *bee hoon*. Afterwards, the whole family would tuck in, communal style, eating the *bee hoon* directly from the serving platter so quickly that the empty plate was still hot when its contents had been devoured.

Papa began to cook more frequently when I was a teenager. Mama would prepare the ingredients for him so that he could simply take over when he came home early from work. He also started to cook more regularly on Sundays. He learned to cook hawker food like fried Hokkien Mee and Loh Mee from Ah Peh and

continuously. As if by magic, swirls of the cooked eggs appeared in the gravy giving it a lovely marbled look. The other thing that made Papa's Loh Mee special was his fried fish topping. He either used leftover fish or steamed a couple of *selar*, flaked the fish meat and fried it with oil, shallots and garlic before seasoning it with light soy sauce and pepper. The meat was fried until it was crispy and, when eaten with the Loh Mee, was unbelievably good.

Papa approached cooking like an art form. He didn't just cook so we could have something to eat, but had the pleasure of coaxing the best out of the ingredients used. He added creative touches to the food he cooked, right down to the way ingredients were prepared. Even the cooking of vegetables, such as *kailan*, was elevated to a loving ritual. He washed the *kailan* leaf by leaf under running water, shook off the excess water and then spread the leaves out in a large colander to dry. When the *kailan* was dried to his satisfaction, he would fry them with his usual flair.

Whether frying vegetables, *bee hoon*, an omelette or cooking a curry, Papa always insisted that enough oil had to be added. He lived in the days when dieting was a laughable notion. People then were not concerned about health problems caused by an abundance of rich food. When you were poor, scrumptious food was an indulgence – an extravagance even; it was considered your good fortune to be able to eat well. He often said, "If you can eat, just eat; why worry so much?" He had no qualms about the liberal amount of oil he used. In fact, he often lamented that we

Hua Mama. There was one occasion when he cooked something called Her Mee, literally "fish noodles". Papa told us that Her Mee used to be sold only by roadside hawkers since making it was so labour-intensive that no one made it at home. The noodles were made of fish meat which Papa scrapped from what we called *huang zhi her* (yellowtail). The meat was then pounded into a paste and mixed with salt and tapioca flour to form a dough. He then rolled it out to a rectangle before rolling it up loosely and cutting it into thin strips, much like making pasta. The fish noodles were cooked in boiling water and tossed in a mixture of lard, soy sauce, sambal chilli, black vinegar and fried shallots, exactly like Tah Mee. That was the only time I ate Her Mee. I appreciated the way Papa was willing to spend that amount of time and effort to make it for us.

I must also tell you about Papa's Loh Mee. I vividly remember him adding beaten eggs to the braised meat gravy that he had already thickened with corn flour. He poured the eggs into the gently bubbling gravy while stirring

THIS PAGE: *Papa cooking for a Sunday get-together dinner at Yee Mama's.*
FACING PAGE: *Papa on one of his fishing trips.*

didn't use lard and extolled its virtues: how food tasted so much better fried with lard than with vegetable oil! To find a happy medium, Papa continued to fry with lard but added an equal amount of vegetable oil to achieve a healthier balance.

In contrast to his use of lard, Papa treated the use of monosodium glutamate with disdain. Sometimes, after a meal at Ah Mm's place, he would complain of being thirsty because of the monosodium glutamate in her cooking. He accepted its inevitable presence in hawker food but refused to use it in his own cooking except when he made fishballs. I think he might have been told by whoever taught him to make the fishballs that monosodium glutamate and salt help impart a springy texture. However, he was not opposed to using oyster sauce; I suspect he was unaware that the flavour enhancer in the oyster sauce is monosodium glutamate! When he fried Hokkien Mee, he would boil a big pot of *ikan bilis* stock with lots of prawns to add flavour to the noodles. There was not a trace of monosodium glutamate in his Hokkien Mee.

Papa was quite the perfectionist; he was finicky to the point of obsession. For example, he spent an inordinate amount of time sharpening his chopper, testing the already razor-sharp edge of the blade with his thumb, then sharpening again and again until he was satisfied. He took enormous pride in cutting translucent slices of carrots and shallots. His forte was cutting ginger into strands so thin they were like hair. We loved eating these ginger strings which he fried in sesame oil until they were golden brown and fragrant. He was also particular about the freshness of ingredients and would only steam fish that was bought from the wet market that same day.

Papa was the first person in his family to actually enjoy eating bread. He used to regularly meet with his good friend after dinner, buy a couple of freshly-baked baguettes and eat them, enjoying the crispy chewy crust and all.

Papa didn't have much of a sweet tooth. Other than adding sugar in coffee and eating sweet potato soup, he totally ignored sweet things like pastries, cakes and pies. Even Chinese pastries like Tau Sah Piah and mooncakes didn't tempt him. So, it was strange that when I was much older, he actually tried his hand at baking! He only baked two types of cake: a plain butter cake and a chocolate butter cake.

Retiring from his work as a car mechanic afforded him the luxury to do what he loved, which was cooking. I learned a lot simply by watching him as he washed vegetables, sliced pork, chopped chicken, cut ginger, minced garlic and fried *bee hoon*. I guess I didn't have much in the way of distraction  then, like cable television or a game console, so watching my Papa cook was both entertaining and educational. When eventually I had to do all these tasks, I found that I already had the know-how.

Fried Kailan

Of all the vegetables Papa cooked, *kailan* or kale, was my absolute favourite. Being a perfectionist in the kitchen, he was always drilling into my head the four unbendable rules about stir-frying leafy greens: firstly, the wok must be smoking hot; secondly, never ever add water to the vegetables unless they are too dry, even then, it should be a sprinkling of just one or two teaspoons; thirdly, always add enough oil to coat and lubricate each leaf or stem of the vegetables or they will taste very *see-ahb* (astringent). Finally, make sure to never overcook them. Papa looked with disdain upon *kalian* and *chye sim* that had been cooked to death in a pool of water, their sprightly green turned a dull, lifeless shade and with insufficient oil to boot.

200 g baby *kalian* (kale)

4 dried shitake mushrooms

2 tablespoons oil

2 cloves garlic, finely minced

12 medium prawns, shelled and deveined

1 tablespoon oyster sauce

Soak the shitake mushrooms until they are soft and plump. Remove them but do not squeeze out the water from the mushrooms; you want to retain some of the liquid so they are moist and juicy. Slice each mushroom into 4 pieces and set them aside.

The baby *kalian* I use here are the oval shaped ones with the shortest of stems. Discard the outer leaves if they are yellowish. Cut each baby *kalian* into half or into quarters lengthwise if they are too big. Wash them under running water, separating the leaves slightly to allow water to flow in between. Shake off as much water as you can and drain the *kalian* well.

Heat the oil in a non-stick wok and sauté the mushrooms until they turn a deep golden brown on each side. This frying deepens and intensifies the flavour of the mushrooms so don't rush through it. Remove the mushrooms and set them aside. Sauté the minced garlic in the remaining oil until the garlic turns golden brown. Add the prawns, stirring continuously until they are almost cooked. Remove the prawns and set them aside with the mushrooms. Now add the *kalian* to the hot wok, stir continuously while adding the mushrooms and oyster sauce. This dish should be slightly moist but without a gravy. If it is too dry, add a tablespoon of water. Stir the whole lot vigorously for 10 seconds; add the prawns, stir again to mix and the dish is done. Turn off the flame immediately so the *kalian* doesn't get overcooked and will still retain its crunchiness.

Seafood Vermicelli

serves 4

I use Chilli Brand rice vermicelli for this recipe. The thin Thai *bee hoon* that is so good fried just doesn't work as well in this recipe. Unlike Papa, I cannot be bothered to cook this for a late night supper; instant noodles will have to do if I want something hot and savoury at night.

200 g *bee hoon*
  (rice vermicelli)
12 medium prawns
1 medium squid
4 stalks *chye sim*
  (mustard greens)
2 cups canned
  chicken stock
3 tablespoons light soy
  sauce
2 tablespoons corn flour
2 eggs
3 tablespoons oil
8 cloves garlic,
  finely minced
White ground pepper
Pickled green chillies
Water

Soak the *bee hoon* in water until it is soft. Drain the *bee hoon* and set it aside. Wash the prawns, cut off the long feelers but leave them unshelled. Remove the head of the squid. Skin the squid and discard everything you find in its cavity. Wash the squid well and cut the body into rings and the head and tentacles into smaller pieces. Wash the *chye sim* and cut it into roughly 4-centimetre lengths.

To make the stock, bring the chicken stock, 3 cups of water and 1 tablespoon of light soy sauce to a boil. Lower the flame and add the prawns. Let the prawns cook in the gentle heat until they turn red. Remove them immediately with a slotted spoon or a strainer. Next, poach the squid rings. When they turn opaque white, remove them right away. Let the stock come back to a boil and cook the *chye sim* for about ten seconds then set it aside with the seafood. Mix the corn flour and ¼ cup water together. Break the eggs into another bowl and beat well. Peel the prawns.

Heat the oil in a non-stick wok. Add the *bee hoon* and garlic and fry, stirring frequently until the *bee hoon* turns golden and slightly crispy. This frying step is crucial as it gives this dish that extra special flavour. Once the *bee hoon* has been well fried, drizzle a tablespoon of light soy sauce all over and continue to fry it until it is well mixed with the *bee hoon*.

Now add all of the stock and the remaining tablespoon of light soy sauce. Let everything come to a boil then let the *bee hoon* simmer for a minute so it can absorb the flavourful stock. Add the corn flour mixture and stir well.

Lastly, stir in the beaten eggs until the eggs start to set. The idea is not to cook the eggs until they curdle but to half-cook them so they are still runny which will help to thicken the sauce. Taste, and add more soy sauce if preferred. Transfer the *bee hoon* onto a big platter or individual plates. Top with the seafood, *chye sim* and dashes of pepper. Serve the *bee hoon* right away with pickled green chillies.

Sin Chew Bee Hoon

FRIED VERMICELLI SINGAPORE STYLE

Papa no doubt ate this Sin Chew *bee hoon* at some *zhi char* (literally, cook and fry) stall and then came home to cook his version for us. I cannot cook this *bee hoon* in exactly the same way Papa did because his cast-iron wok was much bigger than the non-stick one I have. He would fry the *bee hoon* with vegetables first, then pushed the *bee hoon* to the side of the wok to make a space in the centre; he would then add some more oil to sauté the garlic before adding the prawns and soy sauce. After stirring the prawns around for a few minutes, he would stir in the *bee hoon* and fry the whole lot together until the prawns were just cooked. My small wok doesn't allow me to use this method so I have to adapt by cooking the prawns separately.

200 g *bee hoon*
  (rice vermicelli)
250 g prawns, shelled and
  deveined
200 g cabbage
½ small carrot, peeled
100 g *char siew*
  (barbecued pork)
1 large onion, peeled
8 cloves garlic, minced
3½ tablespoons oil
2 eggs
1 tablespoon light soy
  sauce
3 tablespoons oyster sauce
Ground white pepper
¼ cup water
2 cups bean sprouts
Red chillies
Pickled green chillies

Soak the *bee hoon* in plenty of water for about 40 minutes and then drain it. Use kitchen scissors to snip the *bee hoon* into shorter strands so that it is easier to fry. Meanwhile, thinly slice the cabbage. Cut the carrot and *char siew* into thin strips. Cut the onion into ½ centimetre thick slices. Mince the garlic and get the prawns ready.

Heat ½ tablespoon of the oil in a non-stick wok. Scramble the eggs in the oil only till they are soft since they will be cooked further when they are added to the noodles. Transfer the eggs to a bowl and set aside. Add 1½ tablespoons of the oil to the wok. Put in half of the minced garlic and sauté for few seconds. Now add the *bee hoon* and fry, making sure to stir well until the *bee hoon* is very well fried and browns a little. The *bee hoon* tends to clump together. So, a pair of wooden chopsticks, in addition to the wok-fryer, would be very handy for turning the *bee hoon* and loosening the strands. When the *bee hoon* has been thoroughly fried, transfer it to a plate and set it aside.

Now add the remaining 1½ tablespoons of oil to the wok. Sauté the remaining garlic until it turns golden. Add the prawns and stir-fry them quickly until they are almost cooked. You don't want to completely cook the prawns at this stage as they will be cooked again when added to the *bee hoon* later. Transfer the prawns to a plate. Fry the onions, cabbage and carrot in the remaining oil and garlic. Add the light soy sauce, oyster sauce and a dash of white pepper. Let the vegetables cook for a few minutes, longer if you prefer them softer.

Now return the *bee hoon* to the wok and combine it with the vegetables. Again, the long wooden chopsticks would be invaluable in this task. Add the water. Stir again to mix well. If the *bee hoon* is too dry, add one or two tablespoons more water. Now add the bean sprouts; they only need about 10 seconds of mixing to be cooked. Lastly return the prawns and eggs to the wok and fry together with the *bee hoon* for a few more seconds to cook the prawns. Transfer the *bee hoon* to a platter or individual plates. Serve with sliced red chillies or pickled green chillies (or both if you like).

Hokkien Mee

FRIED NOODLES HOKKIEN STYLE   serves 4

I have been disappointed every single time I ordered Hokkien Mee in a hawker centre or food court: the taste of monosodium glutamate overwhelms everything else on the plate. In my younger days, the only fried Hokkien Mee I ate was either cooked by Papa or bought from his hawker friend. This hawker friend was one of a kind: he fried the noodles sitting behind the roaring fire and the huge wok. His Hokkien Mee also came wrapped in a large piece of *opeh* (the base of a palm leaf) which definitely added a certain fragrance to the noodles. But the special taste of his Hokkien Mee had to be due to other reasons that only he knew.

Papa's Hokkien Mee was also special in its own way: there was absolutely no artificial flavour enhancer in the prawn stock. The flavour of the stock came from simmering fried prawn shells, the prawn meat and ikan bilis, with plenty of garlic. He would patiently fry the yellow noodles and thick *bee hoon* until they became so fragrant with the smell of the oil and garlic before adding the stock. He really took pride in frying the Hokkien Mee well and I guess his best reward was watching how we ravenously devoured it. For this recipe, I have used a big squid. I know it's quite a lot for 4 people but I love the thick juicy rings that it yields. I keep the head and tentacles for another dish.

Many hawkers serve *sambal belacan* with their fried Hokkien Mee. I don't because serving *sambal belacan* with this Hokkien Mee would be like asking for ketchup to go with your French food.

400 g fresh yellow noodles
400 g fresh thick *bee hoon*
   (rice vermicelli) 200 g
prawns (about 12
   fairly large ones)
1 big squid, about 250g
4 cups water
4 eggs
100 g pork belly
3 tablespoons oil
200 g bean sprouts
2 tablespoons fish sauce
50 g chives
¼ teaspoon white pepper
8 cloves of garlic
4 calamansi limes, halved
   and deseeded
1 red chilli, sliced

FOR THE PRAWN STOCK
200 g prawns
1 cup split and boneless
   ikan bilis (whitebait)
6 cloves of garlic, sliced
2 tablespoons oil
1 cup water

Heat the 4 cups of water till it comes to a boil. In the meantime, wash and drain the prawns. Remove the head and skin of the squid. Cut the squid into half crosswise, remove the guts and wash the squid well. When the water boils, lower the heat and blanch the squid and the prawns, stirring for about 2 minutes in barely simmering water. Remove the prawns and the squid. Let the prawns cool slightly before shelling and deveining them. Reserve the shells and heads for the prawn stock. Slice the squid into rings. Put the prawns and squid rings on a plate.

To prepare the stock, shell the other 200 g of prawns. Reserve the shells and heads. Set the shelled prawns aside. There is no need to devein these. Put the *ikan bilis* in a strainer, wash under running water and drain well. Slice the garlic. Heat 2 tablespoons of oil in a wok. Add the prawn shells and heads from all the prawns. Stir once to coat the shells with oil and fry till the undersides brown in patches. Now throw in the sliced garlic and turn the shells to brown the other sides. Add the raw shelled prawns, *ikan bilis* and the water used to blanch the prawns and squid. Bring everything to a roaring boil, then lower the heat and add the piece of pork belly to the broth. Cover the wok and simmer for 30 minutes.

Remove the pork and drain the stock into another pot. Now add a cup of water to the prawn meat and *ikan bilis* which still have plenty of flavour in them. Boil this for a few seconds and turn off the flame. Drain this second batch of stock into the same pot containing the first batch. Discard the stock ingredients, including the prawn meat which, by now, would be tasteless. You will have about 4-4½ cups of stock. Slice the pork thinly and set aside with the prawns and squid.

Wash and drain the bean sprouts. Wash the chives and cut them into 5-cm lengths. Mince the garlic.

Heat 1 tablespoon of oil in a non-stick wok. Break the eggs into a bowl and pour all the eggs at once into the wok. Scramble the eggs till they are almost cooked. Return the eggs to the bowl.

Reheat the stock over a small flame as you begin to fry the noodles. Heat the remaining 2 tablespoons of oil till it is very hot and add the yellow noodles, *bee hoon* and garlic all at once. Fry all these together, mixing very well, for at least 5 minutes before sprinkling the 2 tablespoons of fish sauce over the noodles. Continue to fry for another 5 minutes by which time the garlic would have browned and the noodles would have become drier and very fragrant. The dry noodles would be able to absorb the stock much better without turning soggy. Add the eggs and mix them well into the noodles.

Now add most of the stock (leaving about ¾ cup) to the noodles. Immediately cover the wok and let the noodles braise for about ten seconds before stirring. Continue to cook uncovered till the noodles have absorbed most of the stock. Add the chives and sprouts and fry for 10 seconds to mix them well with the noodles.

Serve on a big platter or on individual plates, topped with the prawns, squid and pork. Pour the remaining stock over the noodles to moisten the dish and serve immediately with the calamansi limes and red chilli.

Papa's Instant Noodles

serves 1

Papa did not cook instant noodles with the packet of seasoning provided in the instant noodle carton. Like most of his other specialties, he had his own way of cooking this dish.

1 packet Myojo instant
  noodles
2 cloves garlic, minced
6 prawns, shelled and
  deveined
1 cup water
½ tablespoon oyster sauce
½ tablespoon oil
½ tablespoon light soy
  sauce
1 egg
A dash of pepper

Heat the oil in a non-stick wok. Add the garlic and sauté until it turns golden brown. Add the prawns and stir them around very briefly. You don't want the prawns to be completely cooked at this stage as you will be adding the prawns to the hot noodles later for a bit more cooking. Stir until they are almost cooked. Remove the prawns.

Add the water to the remaining oil and garlic in the wok. Put in the noodles but do not add the seasoning provided in the packet. Include the oyster sauce and light soy sauce. Let everything come to a boil, then lower the heat and let the noodles simmer for a minute. Taste a strand of noodles to check if it is done to the texture of your liking. I prefer my noodles with a little bit of bite. To make softer noodles, simmer them a little longer. Add the egg and immediately stir it into the noodles. It just takes a few seconds for the egg to cook. Stir in the prawns. Turn off the flame. Add a dash of pepper and stir to mix. Transfer the noodles to a plate.

Steamed Squid

serves 4

Whenever Papa managed to get the freshest, big, thick squid, he would simply steam and eat it with a dip of *taucheo* (salted soybean) and a generous heap of roughly chopped coriander leaves and stems. For me, this dish is a celebration of simplicity, both in its preparation and its taste. This steamed squid eaten with watery plain porridge is a classic Teochew dish. With just three ingredients, each holding its own, this dish creates a burst of flavours and textures in the mouth. The intense saltiness of the *taucheo* (I use the light brown version) brings out the sweetness of the squid while the refreshing crunch of the coriander contrasts pleasantly against the slightly chewy bite of the meaty seafood.

1 large squid, about 500 g
2 tablespoons *taucheo*
  (salted soy beans), beans
  and the liquid
2 stalks of coriander,
  leaves and stems

Remove the head and skin of the squid. Cut out the eyes and the ink bag. Wash the head, tentacles and body of the squid well. Put the squid with the head and tentacles on a plate and steam for 4-5 minutes.

Wash the stallks of coriander then roughly chop the leaves and stems. Put the *taucheo* in a small bowl.

Once the squid is steamed, use a fork or a pair of chopsticks to remove the squid from the plate, draining the juices into a bowl. Do be careful as the squid cavity contains some very hot juices released by the squid. Slice the body into rings, cut the tentacles into shorter lengths and the head into quarters. Return the cut squid to the plate, pour the squid juice over, top with the chopped coriander and serve at once with the *taucheo*.

Fried Red Snapper

For this recipe, I use a big red snapper but you can use just about any fish like pomfret, yellowtail or sea bass. You can also fry several smaller fish or, if you don't want to deal with so many bones, then one or two pieces of fillet would do just as nicely. To cut the ginger into very thin strips, you will need a really sharp knife.

1 red snapper, about 800 g
1 piece half-palm size
    young ginger
4 tablespoons sesame oil
½ teaspoon light soy sauce
1½ cups oil
1 teaspoon salt
1 big clove garlic, sliced

Clean the red snapper and dry well with kitchen towels. Make 2 diagonal cuts into the flesh on both sides of the fish to enable the fish to cook faster. Cut the ginger into very thin strands; you should get about a cup. Heat the sesame oil in a non-stick wok and fry the ginger until they turn golden brown and crispy. Sprinkle the half-teaspoon of light soy sauce over the ginger and stir. Remove the ginger with a slotted spoon or metal strainer and transfer onto a kitchen towel to drain off any excess oil.

Add the 1½ cups of oil to the remaining sesame oil in the wok. While the oil is heating up, season the fish on both sides and the stomach cavity with the teaspoon of salt. When the oil is smoking hot, slide the fish into the oil and fry for about 5 to 6 minutes on each side. The fish should turn a beautiful golden brown. Add the garlic slices to the oil during the last few minutes of frying. Put the fish on a rack to drain off the excess oil then transfer it to a plate. Top with fried ginger strings.

Loh Bak

Papa and Mama cooked Loh Bak quite often as it required little preparation. They usually cooked a big pot, enough for dinner with some leftover for lunch the next day. Sometimes, Papa even added pieces of *taukwa* (soya bean cake) to be braised together with the pork. Often, Mama used the leftover pork gravy to prepare a cabbage dish and an egg dish (see page 138 for recipes).

2 strips of pork belly,
    about 250 g each
4 hardboiled eggs, shelled
4 cloves of garlic, peeled
    and smashed
2 tablespoons superior
    dark soy sauce
1 teaspoon salt
2 tablespoons oyster sauce
¼ teaspoon ground white
    pepper
1 small piece cinnamon bark
½ piece of star anise
2 cloves
4 cups water
¼ cup corn flour
½ cup water
Coriander sprigs (optional)

Wash the pork belly well. Remove any hair on the skin with a pair of tweezers. Cut each strip of pork belly into two so they fit in the pot. Put the pork, eggs, garlic, 4 cups of water, dark soy sauce, salt, oyster sauce, pepper, cinnamon bark, star anise and cloves in a large pot. Stir until the dark soy sauce and oyster sauce are evenly mixed. Bring to a boil, then let it simmer tightly covered for about 2 hours until the pork is tender.

Remove the pork and eggs from the sauce. Skim off the fat from the sauce. Reheat the sauce while you mix together ½ cup of water and ¼ cup of corn flour. Add this to the sauce, stirring until the sauce starts to bubble again. Taste and adjust the seasoning if required. Turn off the flame and set the sauce aside.

When the pork has cooled enough to be handled, slice it into pieces about 1-centimetre thick. Cut the eggs into quarters. Arrange the pork and eggs on a large platter. Spoon some of the sauce over and garnish with the coriander leaves.

Loh Mee

BRAISED NOODLES

Once you have learned how to cook Loh Bak (page 85), preparing Loh Mee is the next logical step. The Loh Mee we eat at hawker centres is served with sliced braised pork and a few slices of Ngoh Hiang (meat rolls). Papa's version is extra special. He topped the Loh Mee with fried fish flakes which complement the other ingredients in this dish perfectly. This recipe makes more than enough fish flakes for the Loh Mee, but it makes no sense to cook a smaller quantity, as it requires the same amount of work. Serve the extra fish flakes with rice.

FOR THE FRIED FISH FLAKES
2 *selar* (scad),
   about 200 g each
4 shallots, peeled
2 cloves of garlic, peeled
2 tablespoons oil
¼ teaspoon salt
¼ teaspoon ground
   white pepper
2 teaspoons light soy sauce
¼ teaspoon superior
   dark soy sauce
4 teaspoons castor sugar

FOR THE LOH MEE
600 g fresh yellow noodles
100 g bean sprouts
1 egg, beaten
1 stalk of chinese celery
1 red chilli, deseeded
Fried shallots
Ground white pepper
Black vinegar (optional)

Make Loh Bak (page 85). While the Loh Bak is simmering, prepare the fish flakes. When you buy the *selar*, tell the fishmonger not to scale the fish so that you can easily peel the skin off after steaming them. Wash the fish thoroughly and dry them well. If they are chilled, allow the fish to come to room temperature before steaming them. Place the *selar* in a steaming dish. Heat the steamer and, when it is ready, steam the fish for 5 minutes over high heat. Remove the fish and cool. Reserve the juices.

Peel the skin from the fish and extract the fish meat. Be careful to remove all bones. Flake the fish meat. You should get about 2 cups of flaked fish meat. Add the juices from steaming the fish to the fish meat.

Slice the shallots thinly and finely mince the garlic. Heat the oil in a non-stick wok and fry the shallots for about half a minute until they are soft. Add the garlic and fry for a few seconds (the shallots and garlic don't have to be golden brown at this point). Include all the fish meat with the juices and stir to mix well. Mix in the salt, pepper, light soy sauce and dark soy sauce. Fry the fish flakes over a medium flame until they are well browned and crispy, stirring every half a minute or so. Now add the sugar and stir for a few more seconds. Transfer the fried fish to a bowl and set aside.

Prepare the garnishes for the Loh Mee by chopping the Chinese celery finely and slicing the chilli thinly. When the Loh Bak is done, transfer the pork and the eggs from the gravy to a plate to cool slightly. Slice the pork and the eggs. You can do all the preparation to this point in advance.

To serve the Loh Mee, reheat the Loh Bak gravy over a low flame. When the gravy boils, turn off the flame and immediately add the beaten egg while stirring to create the egg swirls. Cover to keep the gravy hot.

Bring a pot of water to a boil. Once the water boils, throw in all the bean sprouts and blanch for just a couple of seconds. Strain the bean sprouts and set them aside. Divide the noodles into 4 portions. When the water comes back to a boil, blanch one portion of the noodles for about 5 seconds. Drain the noodles and transfer to a serving bowl. Repeat with the other 3 portions of noodles. Divide the bean sprouts among the 4 bowls of noodles and top with sliced pork and eggs. Ladle the hot gravy into each bowl. Garnish each bowl with celery leaves, fried shallots, a dash of white pepper, 1 tablespoon of fish flakes and a few slices of chilli. Add a splash or two of black vinegar for those who like Loh Mee with it.

Bak Ynee

TEOCHEW MEATBALLS   **serves 4**

When Papa decided to make these Bak Ynee, he would get up early that morning and make a trip to the market to buy the freshest *bearh ghah* (*selar*, horse mackerel) or *huang zhi her* (yellowtail). He then spent the better part of the morning cleaning and scraping the fish before pounding the meat in a pestle and mortar with salt, water and a bit of corn flour to make fish paste. After that, he mixed the fish paste with minced pork, little cubes of pork fat, chillies and Chinese celery. The paste is then formed into longish cylindrical shapes to be steamed just in time for our lunch of Teochew porridge.

While Papa was occupied with making the Bak Ynee, Mama would cook the porridge and prepare one or two vegetable dishes. When we sat down to lunch, we all knew the highlight of the meal was Papa's homemade Bak Ynee. My version here is not entirely homemade. I use ready-made fish paste from the Yong Tau Foo seller at the wet market to speed up the process. I have also left out those cubes of pork fat because I don't like the taste.

400 g fish paste
1 red chilli, deseeded
100 g minced pork
¼ cup chopped Chinese
    celery
Dash of ground white
    pepper

Finely dice the chilli. Put all the ingredients in a bowl and mix well using a rubber spatula. There is no need to add any salt or light soy sauce as the fish paste is already well salted. Divide the paste into 8 portions.

Prepare a steamer. Line a round baking tin with non-stick baking paper. Get ready a bowl of water. Wet your hands well to prevent the meat paste from sticking to your hands. Form each portion of meat paste into a roll 8-10 cm long and place it on the non-stick baking paper in the tin. When you have shaped all the meat paste, start to boil the water in the steamer. Once steam begins to escape, steam the meat rolls over high heat for 5 to 6 minutes.

Remove the meat rolls from the steamer. Reserve the juices from steaming the meat rolls. It is very good with porridge.

Slice the meat rolls into approximately 1-centimetre thick pieces. The steamed Bak Ynee tastes wonderful as they are, but if you like, you can enhance the flavour by frying them in some oil until they turn golden brown.

Soups & Night Porridge

I think of Yee Mama as someone full of tenderness and grace. She always maintains her poise and dignity. Looking at her, you wouldn't have guessed that she once led a hard, tragic life.

Yee Mama was born Chew Soo Khim in 1919 in the Teochew region of Tneoh Nge-onh, Guangdong province. Her father sailed to Singapore in search of a job in order to support his family. Back in China, increasing civil unrest caused Yee Mama's mother to fear for the family's safety. She then made the difficult decision of bringing her children and her mother-in-law to Singapore to join her husband.

Once reunited with his family, my great-grandfather rented a room for four dollars a month in an attap house in the Hougang area, then known as "Five Milestone". There were four rooms in that attap house, each occupied by a different family; everyone shared the common living room and kitchen. Although my great-grandfather had been in Singapore for a while, he was unable to get a job. The family therefore had to live an extremely frugal existence.

A particular incident from their early days in Singapore stood out in Yee Mama's mind. One evening, my great-grandmother cooked some shark meat for dinner. Yee Mama was the only one who didn't eat any. The next morning, she woke up to find her family seemingly unconscious in bed with high fever. She immediately ran to a neighbour for help. Upon questioning Yee Mama, the neighbour suspected that her family had been poisoned by the shark meat. He sent Yee Mama to get some green *ghah-nah* (olives) and brown sugar to make an antidote. Gripped by fear, Yee Mama ran to the market, wondering what would happen to her if her family were to die. With the neighbour's help, she boiled the *ghah-nah* liquid and fed it to each of her loved ones. Miraculously, they regained consciousness and the fever gradually left them. Yee Mama even buried the leftover shark meat deep in the ground to prevent any scavenging animal from consuming it.

Shortly after recovering from the poisoning, my great-grandfather, being literate, found work as a clerk with a rice merchant. He drew a salary of $30 a month. On top of this, he received free rice for the family!

A couple of years later, Yee Mama's family was able to move to their own place: a little wooden house with a well. They paid six dollars in rent per month and lived there for two years before moving to Wang Ghairh Suanh Kah (the Clark Quay area) when Yee Mama was thirteen.

After the family had settled, my great-grandmother gave birth to three other daughters and one son who died shortly after birth. Being the eldest daughter in the family, Yee Mama naturally had to help out with all the household chores, including cooking which she learned from her mother. In fact she had to take over all the cooking during her mother's confinement periods. Despite all these responsibilities, Yee Mama was still able to go to school for a few months. She was very happy to attend classes, learning simple Chinese characters and listening to the stories told by the teacher. However, my great-grandfather, eventually conforming to the tradition that girls should stay at home

to learn the ropes of domesticity, stopped Yee Mama's schooling, allowing only her brother to continue with his education.

At home, Yee Mama had her hands full doing chores like cleaning, washing, cooking and looking after her younger siblings. She cooked both porridge and rice for all three meals of the day. Everyone could choose to eat either the porridge or rice; any leftovers were kept for the next meal.

There was no refrigeration in those days, so any remaining stews or soups to be kept for breakfast the next day had to be brought to the boil again just before Yee Mama retired for the night. This was to prevent the food from turning bad. The next morning, once the charcoal fire was ready, these stews or soups were boiled again before being served. Lunch was a slightly more elaborate meal as Yee Mama or my great-grandmother would have had gone to the market to buy fresh meat, fish and vegetables for the day. There were a few of the usual *zahb khiam* and one or two more dishes that could be quickly prepared like steamed fish, omelette and stir-fried vegetables. Dinner was probably the best meal of the day as there was more time to prepare dishes that required slow braising or stewing, like pork intestines and tongue stewed with lily buds or sometimes with *kiam chye* (salted mustard greens). In addition, there was usually a soup; Yee Mama learned to cook omelette soup (page 103) from her mother. Other soups she cooked were *gao nee* meatball soup and pork ribs with black beans soup. Occasionally she would cook

THIS PAGE: *Clarke Quay, where Yee Mama's family lived.*
FACING PAGE: *Yee Mama, aged eighteen.*

a one-dish meal like Hiang See Poong (rice with salted black beans, page 105)

My great-grandfather had the habit of eating what we call *mairh muairh*, meaning night porridge. I guess it was so called because porridge was invariably eaten for supper, unlike the wide choices we have today. Yee Mama would cook some porridge, enough for whoever wanted to eat it. As it was the last meal of the day, she did not prepare elaborate side dishes. The porridge was simply served with fried salted fish or thinly sliced pieces of grilled Chinese sausages.

In those days, there was not much to do for entertainment. Being a teenager, Yee Mama was much too old to be running around playing catch or other such games that little children played. Looking out of the window at the lively street scene was her only form of amusement. Still, proper young ladies were not supposed to blatantly open windows and stare at the goings-on outside. They had to discreetly peek through the gaps of the window slats and secretly watch the street vendors below hawking their wares, people buying fresh produce or sitting on stools eating at the itinerant hawker stalls. Yee Mama can remember buying sweet desserts like black sesame seed paste, Hong Zhou Lor Mai Tzok (red dates with glutinous rice porridge) and almond tea, without ever having to step out onto the street. When she spied her favourite dessert hawker approaching, she would wrap money in a piece of paper and place it inside a tiffin carrier. She lowered the carrier down to the hawker and called out her order. The hawker took the money and checked that the sum was correct before filling the tiffin carrier with what had been ordered. Once the food was hoisted up carefully and the windows were tightly closed, Yee Mama would sit back to enjoy the delightful desserts. Sometimes fresh vegetables, fish and pork were also bought in this fashion.

In 1936, at the age of seventeen, Yee Mama got married. My maternal grandfather was actually her next-door neighbour. Although they knew of each others' existence, they did not meet until their wedding day! Both households shared the same tap and the families became acquainted at the common washing area. I can imagine them exchanging information (and gossip too) about their relatives. It was only after my grandfather's family moved away to a bigger residence nearby that my grandfather's mother sent a matchmaker to *phuayh qing*, meaning to discuss marital relations. My grandfather had a reputation of being a studious gentleman. The fact that he was a civil servant making $120 a month made him an attractive prospect. In fact, the matchmaker mentioned that a wealthy man wished to match my grandfather with his daughter, but he rejected the proposal. Instead, my grandfather indicated his interest in Yee

Mama. Yee Mama's mother agreed to the marriage promptly, so, one and a half months later, Yee Mama and my grandfather were married – just like that!

After the wedding, Yee Mama moved in with her in-laws but her newfound marital  bliss was quickly disrupted. Yee Mama's second sister, who was only nine-years-old, contracted an illness and died just twelve days after the wedding. In the year to come, Yee Mama's mother, brother and youngest sister all contracted tuberculosis which also killed many in Singapore during that time. Her brother and sister recovered after treatment, but tragically, Yee Mama's mother succumbed to the disease. A few years later, my great-grandfather also passed away. Tuberculosis continued to tighten its grip on Yee Mama's family: her third sister developed the disease and died at age fifteen while her youngest sister, who recovered from it in her childhood, was afflicted again in her early twenties, after she had gotten married and given birth to a son. She too lost her life to tuberculosis.

Mama was born in 1939, three years after Yee Mama's wedding. The following year, Yee Mama gave birth to another daughter, my Ah Yee. By then, Yee Mama's home was in South Bridge Road; they lived in a house with bathrooms and a kitchen on the ground floor, while the living, dining and bedrooms were upstairs. My grandfather could afford a servant who did all the household chores, leaving Yee Mama just to care for the two young children. She spent her spare time sewing clothes for herself and her daughters on a sewing machine. She also learned to cook Malay food from her mother-in-law who had lived in a kampong in Johor before coming to Singapore.

Yee Mama became quite adept at turning out spicy dishes like Assam Sotong (Tamarind Squid, page 106), Assam Prawns (page 109), Hiahm Bak (Spicy Pork, page 113) and curry chicken. I can recall a dish she cooked using *cheet kahk her* (Malayan shad or *ikan terubok*). This fish was slowly braised for a long time in a spicy, sweet-and-sour broth flavoured with chillies, shallots and *assam* water. The preparation was fairly easy as there was no need to scale or debone the fish. The work was in maintaining the charcoal fire. The slow cooking process caused the scales and bones to become so soft that they practically dissolved in the gravy. You eat this fish with all the scales and bones, much like canned sardines. I have a faint memory of the smell of this dish and that of the grey-white charcoal. I know that I liked the taste even though it was spicy; it was one of my father's favourite dishes. I had wanted to try out this recipe, but unfortunately buying this *cheet kahk her* is a problem: it is quite an uncommon fish these days since few people know how to cook it.

In late 1941, when the Japanese war broke out in Singapore, Yee Mama was pregnant with her third child. Faced with frequent air raids on the city, Yee Mama and my grandfather decided

THIS PAGE: *Yee Mama's husband.*
FACING PAGE: *(top) The family celebrating Yee Mama's birthday at a restaurant; (bottom right) Yee Mama and Mama; (bottom left) Yee Mama and a grandson.*

that it was safer to escape to the outskirts. The family fled to a house in Hougang that was owned by my grandfather's god-brother. In that house, hiding under a bed, Yee Mama gave birth to my Uncle Robert. Yee Mama remembers that the day after Uncle Robert was born, there was a lull in the bombing which allowed her to sleep and rest. However, the air raid quickly resumed and, with that, their anxieties and fears for their lives began all over again.

During the occupation, my grandfather was enlisted to work for the Japanese distributing rice rations. Because of his employment, he could take home more rice than ordinary citizens with their ration cards. Yee Mama's family hence had enough rice to eat throughout the three years of the Japanese Occupation.

In 1945, after the Japanese surrendered and Singapore returned to British rule, my grandfather continued to work as a civil servant. A colonial government job came with privileges; the family was able to live in spacious quarters in Mang Ghah Kah (Whampoa).

Yee Mama gave birth to three more children: my third and fourth aunts and my youngest uncle. The whole family lived quite happily until 1948 when my grandfather contracted tuberculosis and died, leaving Yee Mama to care for their six children and her blind mother-in-law on her own. Yee Mama and the whole family moved into one room in a shophouse on Mosque Street in Chinatown that cost $20 in rent every month. They lived there for the next ten years, with Yee Mama trying to make ends meet by sewing work clothes for plantation workers and trishaw riders. She managed to sew ten pieces a day but each piece earned her only fifteen cents. She often had to sew late into the night as her days were taken up with caring for the children, doing chores, marketing and cooking. Later on, she sewed ladies' garments which were technically

more demanding as there were design elements like pleats, fancy collars and belts. Although this work was more time-consuming, Yee Mama was able to charge more – a dollar and fifty cents per item. During the most difficult of times, Yee Mama worked even harder. She scrimped, saved and lived on as little as possible, rather than resort to borrowing.

You must wonder how two adults and six children could squeeze into a single room. Well, like Yee Mama said, "It was like steaming fish: you line them up, three on the bed and five on the floor. Those who left the house earliest slept closest to the door." For Yee Mama, poverty inspired creativity and resourcefulness. She made her own mattresses by removing the *kapok* stuffing from her own thick mattress, using it to stuff thinner mattresses. Not a single piece of clothing they wore was bought; Yee Mama purchased the material and sewed clothes for the whole family.

Yee Mama fed her children the kind of food she grew up with. As Yee Mama used recipes she learned from her mother-in-law, Mama and her siblings got to enjoy food flavoured with chillies and *belacan* (shrimp paste). No wonder all my aunties and uncles love spicy food. Later on, when Mama and Ah Yee started work, Yee Mama even prepared food for their lunch break. She planned the dishes carefully, cooking stews like Loh Bak, which could be eaten for dinner, and the leftovers reheated for lunch the next day.

Living in a Chinatown shophouse meant that Yee Mama and her family had ample opportunities to sample food from the coffee shops and food stalls downstairs. The family became coffee drinkers and started to eat bread, but only as a light snack. However, they very seldom ate out, as it was much cheaper to cook at home. Only on special occasions did they take away favourite dishes like Hainanese pork chops.

As Mama and her siblings grew older and started working, Yee Mama's financial burden began to ease. When Mama got married, Yee Mama and the other children moved to a flat in Bukit Ho Swee. The room in Mosque Street became my parents' home. It was there that my sisters and I were born.

I have many fond memories of visiting Yee Mama in Bukit Ho Swee. Sometimes, I even stayed there for a week or two so that Mama could have an easier time with one child less to care for. When I accompanied Yee Mama to the wet market, I was excited by the sight of so many items on display, by the bustling crowd

buying, selling, haggling, jostling, chatting and laughing. I held Yee Mama's hand for safety while I took in the scene and watched her buy the items she needed for the day's meals. Would you believe that Yee Mama could afford to eat abalone then? It only cost a dollar and twenty cents per can, though still slightly more costly than other food. Yee Mama cooked the abalone with water chestnuts, mushrooms and pork. This is a dish that Mama rarely cooks since abalones now are so exorbitantly priced. For the same reason, I have not included the recipe in this book.

On Sundays, Yee Mama would not cook the usual weekday fare of porridge for lunch and rice for dinner. Instead, there were Sunday specialties like fried *bee hoon* (vermicelli), fried *mee suanh* (rice vermicelli), curry chicken and even Nasi Lemak (coconut rice).

The feast that stands out most prominently in my mind is the steamboat reunion dinner on Chinese New Year's Day. Mama and all my aunties would help out with the preparation: boiling the soup stock, slicing the liver, pork, fish, chicken meat and abalone; shelling and cleaning prawns and squids; making pork  balls; soaking the *bee hoon* and *tang hoon* (bean vermicelli) and washing a variety of vegetables. There was none of the processed food that people today are so fond of including in their steamboat meals. The charcoal pieces had to be

THIS PAGE: *A snapshot of me, taken outside Yee Mama's flat in Bukit Ho Swee.*
FACING PAGE: *My great-grandmother, Yee Mama's mother-in-law.*

lit and allowed to burn to ash-white before one of my aunties used a pair of long black tongs to pick them up and place them in the funnel of the steamboat. Then there was the table to be set: it was the only time of the year when the whole family sat down at the same time for a meal. My aunties arranged bowls, soup spoons, chopsticks and those cute little gold-coloured metal nets used for fishing cooked pieces of food from the steamboat. They also set small bowls of chilli sauce and light soy sauce for dipping. When all the cutlery and utensils were in place, including pretty glasses and bottles of F&N drinks, Yee Mama and my aunties would bring out the plates of meat and vegetables, and finally the simmering steamboat, which was placed at the centre of the table. I was totally awed by that beautifully set table laden with food.

There were only enough places at the table for the adults, so Mama and one of my aunties cooked the children's share of food for us before all the grown ups crowded in and started the feast. I can remember clearly the smell of the charcoal and the aroma of the bubbling soup. Everyone was chatting, chuckling, enjoying the food and relishing those shared moments of pleasure. It was a scene that filled me with unspeakable warmth and joy.

Today, Yee Mama can put all her heart-breaks and adversities behind. Her children and grandchildren are all grown up; she has a total of seventeen great-grandchildren, with more to come. Although afflicted by ill health, and hence selective about what she eats, she still has a fairly good appetite. She enjoys food like Shark's Fin Soup, *dim sum*, Tah Mee (dry noodles), Duck Rice and Oh Nee (Yam Pudding, page 117). You should see her eat steamed fish: she can expertly reduce a fish into a neat pile of bones, totally picked clean. While we prefer fish fillets, Yee Mama goes for the stomach and the head where most of the bones are, and thoroughly enjoys the process of eating them.

When I visit Yee Mama, we talk about old times. I treasure her dimpled smile as I tell her which of her old recipes I have been cooking for my family.

FACING PAGE: (top) *The table set for the Chinese New Year reunion steamboat dinner;* (bottom) *a regular get-together Sunday dinner at Yee Mama's.*

Cucumber & Meatball Soup

serves 4

Mama learned most of her soup recipes from Yee Mama so we have had our fair share of soups for dinner. However, I didn't like every one of them, like black beans and pork rib soup and any soup made with Chinese herbs. This cucumber and meatball soup was one I loved even though I dreaded the job of mincing the pork and prawns. This is a light, clear soup made with *ikan bilis* (whitebait) stock although you can certainly use canned chicken broth. If you do, you'll only need one cup of canned chicken broth mixed with 3 cups of water.

1 cup split and boneless
   ikan bilis (whitebait)
100 g medium prawns
100 g minced pork
1 teaspoon cornflour
2 teaspoons light soy sauce
Ground white pepper
1 cucumber, about 400 g
4 cups water
Fried shallots
Shallot oil

Put the *ikan bilis* in a sieve and wash under a running tap. Combine the *ikan bilis* and the 4 cups of water in a pot and bring to the boil. Cover the pot and let it simmer for half an hour. Top up with water to replace any that has evaporated during the simmering process. Strain the *ikan bilis* stock into another pot.

Wash the prawns well then shell and devein them. Roughly mince the prawns or cut them into small cubes. Mix the pork, prawns, 1 teaspoon of cornflour, 2 teaspoons of light soy sauce and a couple dashes of ground white pepper together. Set aside.

Cut away and discard the tips of the cucumber. Peel the cucumber and cut it into quarters lengthwise. Remove the seeds in the centre and slice the strips of cucumber on the diagonal to 1-centimetre thick slices. Put the cucumber slices into the strained *ikan bilis* stock and bring to the boil. Cover the pot and let it simmer for about 10 minutes until the cucumber slices are tender. Lower the flame to simmer the soup very gently.

Shape the pork and prawn mixture into 2-cm balls and drop them gently into the soup. You should get about 12 meatballs. Cook the meatballs in the barely simmering soup for about 5 to 6 minutes. Avoid boiling the meatballs vigorously in the soup or they will become very dry. Gently cooking them will ensure that they retain the moisture. Taste, and add light soy sauce if it is needed.

Ladle the soup into individual bowls with the cucumber slices and the meatballs. Add some fried shallots, a few drops of shallot oil and a light dash of ground white pepper.

*

Winter Melon and Egg Soup is a variation of this recipe which replaces the cucumber with 400 g of winter melon. To prepare the winter melon, simply cut off about a 3-millimetre thick layer of the dark green skin. Using your knife, separate the spongy centre with the seeds and discard them. You will be left with a ring of winter melon; cut this up into large cubes or chunks. Add an egg into the soup just after the meatballs are cooked. Stir continuously until the transparent egg turns opaque.

Omelette Soup

serves 4

This was a soup Mama grew up with. It was also the favourite soup of my childhood. Strangely, Mama seldom cooked it, but whenever she did, it was a special treat for me. This isn't the kind of soup that needs hours of simmering. Yee Mama cooked this soup with *ikan bilis* (whitebait) stock, which just takes about half an hour to make.

2 rounded tablespoons
    dried shrimps
2 cups canned chicken
    stock
1 teaspoon oil
1 bundle, about 40 g
    tang hoon (mung bean
    vermicelli)
4 eggs
2 teaspoons light soy sauce
¼ teaspoon ground white
    pepper
3 cups water
1 tablespoon oil
1 stalk coriander leaves

Wash, drain and pound the dried shrimps. Heat 1 teaspoon of oil in a pan or wok. Add the dried shrimps and fry them over a gentle flame, stirring occasionally until the shrimps become fragrant and crispy. Set the fried shrimps aside in a large bowl. While the shrimps are frying, soak the *tang hoon* in hot water for about 5 minutes until they are soft. Cut the *tang hoon* up into roughly 3-centimetre lengths and put these in the bowl together with the fried shrimps. Now break the eggs into the same bowl, add the light sauce and white pepper. Beat the eggs, mixing all the ingredients well.

Heat the chicken stock and water together in a saucepan. Fry the egg mixture in a wok using 1 tablespoon of oil, adding more oil if necessary. You want the omelette to be a deep golden brown as the browning adds another dimension of flavour to the soup. Cut the omelette into bite size pieces with your wok fryer. Add the omelette pieces to the soup and let it come to a boil. Lower the heat and let the soup simmer covered for a couple of minutes to allow the flavours to infuse.

Ladle the soup into individual soup bowls, garnish with a dash of pepper and lots of coriander leaves.

Chives Soup

serves 2

This is a very basic soup made with *ikan bilis* stock and chives, which are inexpensive ingredients, and hence very affordable even in Yee Mama's day. You can use either homemade or canned chicken stock. This soup can be made more substantial by including additional ingredients like prawns, meatballs or soft soya bean cake.

1 cup split and boneless
    ikan bilis (whitebait)
2 cups water
½ tablespoons oil
4 thin slices of ginger
1 garlic, thinly sliced
100 g chives, cut into 3-cm
    lengths

Put the *ikan bilis* in a sieve and wash under running water. Boil the *ikan bilis* in 2 cups of water and cover the pot to let it simmer for about half an hour. Top up the *ikan bilis* stock to replace water that has evaporated during the simmering process.

In another pot, heat the oil to sauté the ginger and garlic slices until they turn golden brown. Pour the *ikan bilis* stock directly into the sautéed garlic and ginger through a sieve. Let the soup come to a gentle boil and lower the heat before adding the chives. Chives cook very quickly; when the soup comes back to a boil again, it is ready. Serve this soup with a dash of pepper.

Hiang See Poong

serves 4

Rice with salted black beans or what we call Hiang See Poong is one of my favourite rice dishes. Yee Mama learned this dish from her mother and cooked it for her children. Mama, in turn, cooked this rice for us when we were growing up but has not prepared it for over twenty years. Just thinking about the distinctive smell of this Hiang See Poong transports me right back to the little kitchen where Mama fried the garlic, salted blacks beans and pork belly that were to be cooked with the rice in the electric rice cooker. There was no outlet in the kitchen to plug in the rice cooker so our rice cooker had to be placed in our one and only bedroom. When the Hiang See Poong was being cooked, the fragrant smell was so distractingly tempting. My sister and I would sometimes lift the lid of the cooker to revel in the aroma even though the orange light on the cooker was still on.

Today, I cook Hiang See Poong in the microwave oven as it can cook rice just as well as a rice cooker. I don't see the need for two kitchen appliances that can perform a similar function, so I have resisted purchasing a rice cooker to this day. Also, straying from tradition, I use pork fillet instead of pork belly, as I don't enjoy eating the skin of the latter. You can get the small packets of salted black beans from the dry goods stalls at the wet market. When pounded, each packet can yield about 3 tablespoons of black bean paste.

3 cups rice, washed
   and drained
3 tablespoons pounded
   salted black beans
500 g medium prawns
200 g pork fillet
5 tablespoons oil
8 cloves garlic, finely
   minced
1 tablespoon light soy
   sauce
1 teaspoon sugar
¼ teaspoon monosodium
   glutamate
3 cups water
1 stalk Chinese celery,
   chopped
1 stalk spring onions,
   chopped
Ground white pepper

Drain and pound the beans to get about 3 tablespoons of black bean paste. Wash the prawns well, then shell and devein them. Slice the prawns into two, lengthwise. Thinly slice the pork fillet into 2- to 3-millimetre thick slices. Wash the black beans in a sieve under running water to get rid of excess salt. Drain well and pound the black beans into a paste. You should have about 3 tablespoons.

Heat 3 tablespoons of oil in a non-stick wok and sauté the salted black bean paste, stirring it to break up the lumps. After about 10 seconds, when it has become fragrant, add half of the minced garlic. Continue to sauté until the garlic browns. Remove half of the black bean paste and garlic mixture and set it aside in a dish. Add the sliced pork fillet to the mixture in the wok and stir until the pork is just cooked. Add the drained rice, light soy sauce, sugar and monosodium glutamate. Stir to mix well. Transfer the rice to a microwave-proof dish. Add the 3 cups of water. Cook the rice (covered) in the microwave oven at a medium setting (540w) for 18 minutes. You can also use a rice cooker.

While the rice is cooking, heat the remaining 2 tablespoons of oil and sauté the rest of the minced garlic. When the garlic browns, add the prawns, chopped spring onions and Chinese celery. Stir continuously until the prawns turn red. Transfer the mixture to a bowl and set aside.

When the rice is cooked, let it sit for about 10 to 15 minutes to ensure that all the rice grains are cooked through. Do this too if you are using an electric rice cooker. Now stir the prawns and the remaining black bean paste and garlic mixture into the rice. Scoop the rice into bowls or plates, add a dash of pepper to the rice and serve immediately.

Assam Sotong

TAMARIND SQUID   serves 4

Assam Sotong is one of the several Malay dishes Yee Mama learned from her mother-in-law. It is very easy and quick to prepare, and goes extremely well with rice. The sweet, savoury, spicy and tangy *assam* gravy is so appetizing.

2 squids, about 200 g each
¼ cup *assam* (tamarind)
   paste 3 stalks lemongrass
4 red chillies, deseeded
6 shallots, peeled
1 cup water
2 tablespoons oil
1½ tablespoons sugar
½ teaspoons salt

Remove the skin, eyes, ink bags and guts from the squids. Wash the squids well; slice the bodies into ½-centimetre thick rings. Cut the head and tentacles up into smaller pieces. Set all the squid aside.

Cut off the leafy parts of the lemongrass, leaving just about 5-centimetre of the root ends. Remove the thick outer parts of the lemongrass and thinly slice the tender interior. Slice also the chillies and shallots thinly. (Keep the tops of the lemongrass in the freezer and use them to flavour curries).

Mix the *assam* paste with the cup of water. Use your fingers to squeeze the paste so that the seeds separate from the pulp. When the pulp has dissolved, strain the *assam* water into a bowl and discard the seeds.

Heat the oil in a non-stick wok and sauté the lemongrass, chillies and shallot slices for about 10 to 15 seconds until they release their fragrances. You don't want to brown the shallots. Add all the *assam* water, sugar and salt. Stir to dissolve the sugar and salt. When the *assam* gravy comes to a boil, put in the squid. Continue to stir until the squid turns opaque. Turn off the flame. Taste and adjust the seasoning, if necessary. Serve with rice.

Assam Prawns

TAMARIND PRAWNS   serves 4

This is another spicy, appetizing dish that partners with rice so well you don't need any other side dishes. Assam Prawns require a bit more work than Assam Sotong as the ingredients have to be pounded. For this dish, I don't recommend grinding the ingredients in a blender as you need to add water to the blender in order to facilitate the grinding. This tends to result in too smooth a puree. I pound the ingredients manually for a coarser texture, giving better mouth-feel to the dish.

500 g medium prawns
¼ cup *assam* (tamarind)
  paste
2 stalks lemongrass
12 shallots
4 cloves garlic
4 red chillies
8 candlenuts
½ tablespoon *belacan*
  (shrimp paste)
1 cup water
3 tablespoons oil
1 tablespoon sugar
½ teaspoon salt

Wash the prawns, then shell and devein them. Set them aside. Remove the leafy part of the lemongrass and use only 5-centimetres of the root end. Don't forget to peel off the thicker outer layers of the lemongrass. Slice the lemongrass, shallots, garlic and chillies to make them easier to pound. Pound these together with the candlenuts and *belacan* until you get a course paste. Remember we don't want a smooth puree.

Mix the *assam* paste with the water. Squeeze the *assam* paste with your fingers and rub the sticky pulp from the seeds so that the pulp dissolves in the water. Strain the *assam* water into a bowl and discard the seeds.

Heat the oil in a non-stick wok and fry the pounded ingredients over medium-high heat for about 5 minutes until very fragrant. Add the *assam* water, salt and sugar. Stir and let the sauce come to a boil. Add the prawns, stirring continuously so the prawns are evenly cooked. The dish is ready once the prawns turn pink and curl up. Serve with rice.

Chilli-Belacan Selar

Whenever Yee Mama fried this fish, the lovely pungent smell of the chilli-*belacan* paste would draw me into the kitchen where I took in a deep lungful of the aroma. However, the fish was too spicy for me then and I could barely taste the fried *selar*. Later, when I was more accustomed to eating chillies, I simply devoured this fish. Mama has not fried this fish for years due to hearsay that *belacan* has high cholesterol content. Although this dish does require an ample amount of *belacan*, I think moderation is the key. Limit yourself to eating this a few times a year. Better a little enjoyment than none at all.

2 *selar* (horse mackerel), about 250 g each
4 red chillies, deseeded
2 cloves garlic
1 tablespoon *belacan* (shrimp paste)
1 cup oil
2 calamansi limes (optional)

Get the fishmonger to gut and scale the *selar* for you. Wash the *selar* well and dry thoroughly with kitchen towels. Cut 3 diagonal slits on each side of the fish and set aside.

Slice the chillies and roughly chop up the garlic to make them easier to pound. Pound the chillies and garlic together with the *belacan* until you get a paste. Insert some of the chilli-*belacan* paste into each of slits in the fish, as well as the stomach cavity.

Heat the oil in a non-stick wok. When the oil is hot, slide the two fishes into the oil and fry over medium to medium-high heat for about 2 minutes on each side. You can cover the wok partially to prevent splattering. The chilli-*belacan* will turn extremely dark brown, almost black but it won't burn unless you fry the fish for too long over very high heat.

As the fish fry, bits of the chilli-*belacan* mixture will stray into the hot oil and be fried to a deep, dark brown. Don't discard these bits of the chilli-*belacan* as they are the best part of this dish. Strain the oil through a sieve and collect these fragrant bits.

Transfer the fish onto a serving plate. Serve with the fried chilli-*belacan* bits and the calamansi limes if desired.

Hiahm Bak

serves 4

For this really tasty dish, you need pork belly. The layers of fat lubricate and moisten the lean meat while the skin provides the gelatinous texture that makes this dish interesting. Those who eat pork belly will really appreciate this. For my own eating pleasure, I use lean pork. I prefer to manually pound the ingredients to get a courser texture for the spice gravy.

200 g pork belly
   or lean pork
1 cup water
12 shallots
4 cloves garlic
8 candlenuts
4 red chillies
½ tablespoon *belacan*
   (shrimp paste)
2 tablespoons oil
½ teaspoon salt

Cut the strip of pork belly into half if it is too long. Put the pork belly in a small pot and add one cup of water. This should be enough to cover the pork. Bring it to a boil, cover the pot and simmer the meat for 30 minutes. Leave the pork to cool in the pot. When it is cool enough to be handled, take the pork out of the pot and slice into ½ centimetre thick slices. Pour the pork stock into a measuring cup and top up with water to make 1 full cup.

Cut or slice the shallots, garlic, candlenuts and chillies to make an easier and faster job of pounding them. Pound these ingredients, together with the *belacan* into a coarse paste.

Heat the oil in a non-stick wok and fry the pounded ingredients over medium-high heat for about 5 minutes until very fragrant and the colour darkens. Stir in the pork slices for a few seconds before adding the 1-cup of pork stock and the salt. Stir and let the pork simmer for about half a minute. Serve with rice.

Green Bean & Rice Soup

Many of us are accustomed to eating green bean soup cooked with sago, but how about green bean soup with glutinous rice? That was the way Yee Mama and Mama cooked green beans. In fact, Yee Mama would cook this for lunch just for a change from the daily porridge, as well as to satisfy her sweet tooth. Occasionally, she even prepared a savoury version by simmering the green beans with just enough water to cover the beans. When the beans were soft, she strained the beans and mixed them with some lard, light soy sauce and ground white pepper. I can imagine that green beans prepared this way would taste somewhat like savoury bean paste (*khiam tau sah*), the filling Hua Mama used for her *kueh*. The recipe here is for the sweet version.

½ cup green beans
¼ cup glutinous rice
4 cups water
½ cup sugar
2 pandan leaves, knotted

Wash the green beans and glutinous rice. Put these in a pot and add the water, sugar and pandan leaves. Bring to a boil, cover the pot and simmer gently for about 45 minutes to an hour.

Leave it to sit for another 15 minutes so the beans and rice are really tender. If too much of the water has evaporated, add more water and return to a boil. Taste to check if it is sweet enough for you, and add more sugar if necessary. Ladle into bowls and serve.

Oh Nee

YAM PUDDING   serves 6-8

This is Yee Mama's favourite dessert and certainly one that I enjoyed tremendously as a child. We usually only ate it on special occasions like weddings or birthday dinners in Teochew restaurants. I remember a few years ago at a cousin's wedding dinner, we were served this dessert. The waitress brought a big bowl of Yam Pudding topped with coconut milk and gingko nuts. Everyone at my table sat looking at that dessert with anticipation while waiting for the waitress to come back with individual serving bowls and a serving spoon. She didn't come back. We noticed that guests at the tables around us were all tucking in communal–style, so, despite feeling a bit awkward, we followed suit. And guess what? It was the best Yam Pudding I ever ate in my life. I think everyone else felt the same since we unashamedly cleaned out the bowl!

I remember the Oh Nee we ate in restaurants long ago came with a gleaming layer of lard on top that was stirred into the dessert. Yee Mama used lard to cook the Yam Pudding too, but I have substituted it with shallot oil. I have also omitted the gingko nuts, which I feel is an unnecessary addition.

1 yam, about 700 g
4 pandan leaves
2 tablespoons shallot oil
½ cup castor sugar
½ cup water (optional),
    or more
1 cup coconut milk

First, put on your rubber gloves. If you're wearing the disposable kind, wear a double layer. You do not want to get that intolerable itch from touching the raw yam with your bare hands.

Start your steamer. Peel the yam; slice it in half lengthwise and then cut each half into 1½ to 2-centimetre thick slices. Arrange the yam slices in a container (a cake tin would do nicely here), allowing a little space between the slices for the steam to circulate. Cut two of the pandan leaves in half and arrange these on top of the yam. Steam the yam for 20 to 30 minutes. Once the yam is steamed, use a spoon to press one or two pieces of yam at a time through a sieve into a mixing bowl. This method of mashing the yam will ensure that you get a very smooth, lump-free pudding. If you find hard bits of yam which are difficult to mash, discard them.

When you have finished pressing all the yam pieces through the sieve, use a measuring cup to measure the amount of yam you have. The recipe for yam pudding here is in the proportion of 1-cup yam to ¼ cup sugar to ¼ cup water. You should be able to get about 2 cups of mashed yam but make any necessary adjustments according to the amount you have. This is not cake baking where you need to be accurate with your measurement of ingredients, you can pretty much go by your personal taste concerning the sweetness and consistency of the Yam Pudding. Add more water if you prefer a more liquid consistency.

To cook the mashed yam, heat the oil in a non-stick wok. Using shallot oil will give an added flavour to the Yam Pudding. Add the mashed yam, sugar, and the remaining 2 pandan leaves tied in a knot. If you like a thick Yam Pudding, omit the water; add more than the ½ cup if your prefer a more liquid consistecy. Stir continuously until the sugar melts and the whole mixture is very well heated through. Remove the pandan leaves. Serve the Oh Nee hot, topped with coconut milk, either in a big serving bowl or in small individual dishes.

Porridge
& Steamed Fish

If I were to name one person whom I am inextricably linked to by food and cooking, it has to be my mother. How could she not be? My earliest memory of being in a kitchen was with her. I was five years old and we were in the communal kitchen of the Mosque Street shophouse. At the time there was no gas stove, so lighting the charcoal fire was a daily chore that had to be started way before the actual cooking began. I enjoyed watching Mama light the charcoal and fan the flames, adjusting the little opening in the stove to let in just the right amount of air to feed the fire. She had it down to a science: too much and there would be an inferno; too little and the flames might die out. I loved watching the pretty orange cinders escaping from the stove into the air and smelling the scent of burning charcoal. Occasionally, Mama would let me fan the flames, warning me not to bend too close to the stove or my hair would catch fire.

My mother, Teo Whee Eng, only received two years of schooling after the end of the Japanese Occupation. She was an excellent student, consistently ranked first or second position in class. Unfortunately, after my grandfather passed away, it was not possible for her to continue schooling. Mama embarked on her own pursuit of self-improvement in culinary skills. When she became a mother, she never took a single day off from her kitchen duties. Even when she was sick she would cook something simple like pork porridge (page 125) for us. It was only when we were older and could purchase food from the hawker centre nearby that she would put off cooking when she was unwell.

One of the first things that Mama allowed me to cook was the brown rice paste for my younger brother. Mama bought the brown rice and had it ground at the Chinese medicine shop. She made the stock by simmering a small handful of *ikan bilis* (whitebait) in about a bowl of water. She then drained the stock and discarded the fish. Next, she poured the stock into an enamel container and added a few spoonfuls of ground brown rice. I helped her stir the mixture until a smooth, soft paste was formed. I had to keep stirring to prevent the rice paste from sticking to the bottom of the little pot. When the gruel had cooled sufficiently, I fed my brother, freeing Mama to do her unending list of chores.

When we moved away from Mosque Street to Joo Seng Road, most of my time was also spent with Mama in the kitchen. I was either

observing how she prepared and cooked meals or helping her out with household chores. When the food was cooked, Mama wanted us to eat while it was hot. She would usually busy herself with the cleaning up or hand-wash the laundry before eating her own meal. It was only when we had whole steamed fish that she would sit at the table to eat with us for the purpose of ensuring that we removed the bones from the fish meat.

Mama watched what we ate quite closely when we were little. She seldom bought sweets or snacks like peanut candy, *siang zah* (haw flakes) or Tau Sah Piah (Bean Paste Cakes). When she did, we were each only given a small amount. For supper, she frequently gave us a cup of hot milk made with a couple of teaspoons of sweet condensed milk diluted with water. She'd let us have a couple of crackers (what we called *soh-dah piah*) to dunk in the milk before eating. She very seldom bought the kind coated with sugar, so you can imagine how my sisters

and I hankered after them. Once in a while, she might buy a tin of Milo or a jar of Horlicks. As for sweet fizzy drinks, we only drank them during Chinese New Year when we went visiting. They were things which Mama never thought of buying when there was no occasion for them. We didn't think of pestering her to do so either.

Mama cooked quite an expansive variety of dishes, but the one thing that will always remind me of Mama is porridge. For us Teochews, there is nothing simpler than a humble bowl of hot, watery plain porridge. It soothes the stomach, assuages the emotions and comforts the soul. As a child, I didn't appreciate this very much. Porridge was simply something we had for lunch practically everyday. It was usually plain, exactly the way Yee Mama and Hua Mama cooked it, and served with two or three side dishes like steamed fish and stir-fried vegetables. We also ate a kind of sweet and salty preserved lemon that was mashed together with a couple of heaping spoonfuls of sugar. I really liked this sweet lemony side dish and was usually so busy eating it that I would forget all about my porridge – which would have earned me a knock on the head from my paternal grandfather if he were there.

Eating such familiar lunches almost daily did breed the occasional discontent, which Mama sometimes dispelled by cooking a fish porridge (page 127) into which she added chunks of carrots, onions, and tomatoes. At other times, she might cook peanut porridge (page 131) or pork porridge (page 125). No wonder, porridge, more than any other food,

THIS PAGE: *My second sister and I.*
FACING PAGE: *Mama and her siblings, Mama when she was 24, Mama and Papa's engagement picture.*

120

evokes powerful nostalgic memories of my childhood.

I have a particularly fond memory concerning my first day of school. I remember Mama waking me up to a cold, dark January morning. As I walked to the little kitchen with half-opened eyes, I saw Papa silhouetted against the dull glow of a single fluorescent light, stirring a pot of porridge, the steam rising and dissipating towards the ceiling. The warm, familiar smell of the porridge permeated the cold morning air. I washed up and changed unenthusiastically; school was a frightening prospect. I didn't want to leave home but Mama had already set a little dish of red preserved bean curd on the table. I had no stomach for food at all and my throat had gone so tight I could hardly swallow. Papa placed a bowl of the steaming

porridge before me, urging me to eat. I have absolutely no recollection of what transpired on that first day in school, but that little kitchen scene stays indelibly in my mind.

Besides porridge, steamed fish was another frequently eaten dish of my childhood. At nearly every lunch, there would be a plate of either whole steamed fish or a fillet. Mama steamed the different types of fish in a variety of ways: with just thinly cut strips of ginger, pieces of tomatoes, spring onions or slices of hydrated Chinese mushrooms. Sometimes, she added *khiam chye* (salty preserved cabbage mustard) or *taucheo* (soya bean paste). It is a wonder I didn't tire of eating steamed fish. To this day, I enjoy it as much as I enjoy fried fish. From a young age, Mama had already taught me how to extract the tender succulent fish meat from the bones with a pair of chopsticks, and how to remove chunks of the meat rather than flake it all up. Today, a bowl of plain porridge and a dish of steamed fish brings me back to a time when my siblings and I squeezed together around our little rectangular dining table, hungrily awaiting dinner.

Mama wasn't the perfectionist like Papa was when it came to cooking, but she was a naturally good cook, creative with whatever ingredients were at hand. She had a knack for serving uncomplicated dishes that took very little time to prepare but yet tasted so good; food like omelette with dark soy sauce, pork fried with *chinchalok* (brined baby shirmps) or scrambled eggs cooked in leftover gravy from Loh Bak (pork braised in dark soy sauce). Sometimes, when we wanted soup but she hadn't prepared any, she'd simply dissolve some Bovril in hot water and season it with lots of ground white pepper. We slurped it all up.

As my siblings and I got older and took less of her time, Mama was able to attend cooking courses at the nearby community centre one night each week to learn new recipes and better her culinary skills. I always waited in great anticipation for her to come home from each lesson as she would bring food prepared by the instructor during his demonstration. Although it just gave us a taste, the small mouthful which each of us got was enough to thrill us. I remember thinking that when I grew up, I wanted to be just like Mama: I wanted to attend cooking classes too, and learn new dishes to cook for everyone.

In the 1980s, Mama bought an oven, a true milestone in the culinary history of our family. It was a silly-looking oven: round and fat like an

inflated flying saucer. Mama was brought up in a Chinese kitchen that traditionally did not have an oven. Still, she developed a taste for cakes, particularly butter cakes. Since my sisters and I had gone through home economics classes in school and learned the fundamentals of simple baking, Mama thought it was time we did some baking right in our own kitchen. Mama relegated the baking to us; she merely enjoyed the fruits of our labour. Our oven was actually underused, as we hadn't learned to roast meats, make casseroles or bake any other pastries. Yet, it was enough to satisfy our cravings for butter cakes. For the first time, our kitchen was filled with the heady and tantalizing aroma of cakes being baked. Mama enjoyed cakes straight from the oven, eating a few slices before waiting for the cake to cool totally.

To this day, Mama has not stopped learn-ing about cookery. She watches cooking programmes on television religiously, and cooks the featured dishes that she thinks we would enjoy. Whenever she eats something good at restaurants, she analyzes the taste, infers the ingredients and seasonings used and attempts to cook it at home. Today, she has no problem cooking an eight-course Chinese dinner, complete with appetizer, shark's fin soup with crabmeat, main courses of prawns, fish, chicken, vegetables, abalone and dessert. She also bakes cakes, pizzas and Chinese New Year cookies. Mama is continually pushing the horizon of her culinary vista.

THIS PAGE: (Top) *Cooking classes at a community centre.* (Bottom) *Mama's oven.*
FACING PAGE: *Mama and I at Haw Par Villa.*

Pork Porridge

Mama usually cooked this pork porridge when she wanted something easy and fuss-free. You can substitute the pork with one chicken breast but the rest of the ingredients are absolutely essential. It is the combination of the egg yolk with the dark soy sauce, sesame oil and pepper that gives this porridge its unique flavour. I don't add wholly dark soy sauce to the porridge because it is too dark and a bit on the sweet side. Instead, I use a combination of dark and light sauces for a more judicial balance. Start with 2 teaspoons of dark and 1 teaspoon of light per bowl. Adjust from there to your taste. Yes, you do need to stir the whole egg into the porridge, as the heat will softly cook the whites while the yolk provides the lovely flavour of this dish.

300 g lean pork, cut into
  1 cm slices
8 cups water
¾ cup rice
4 eggs
Superior dark soy sauce
Light soy sauce
Sesame oil
Ground white pepper

Put the pork and water into a pot and bring it to boil. Meanwhile wash and drain the rice. When the water is boiling, lower the heat and add the rice, stirring occasionally to prevent the rice from sticking to the bottom of the pot. When the porridge starts to bubble, cover the pot and continue to let the porridge simmer gently for about half an hour until the rice grains are disintegrated and very soft. Let the porridge steep for 15 minutes, after which the porridge will thicken considerably and become sticky like congee.

When you are ready to eat, reheat the porridge, stirring to prevent sticking. If it is too thick and difficult to stir, just add a little bit more water. Once the porridge is very hot, ladle it into bowls, break an egg in each, add the dark and light soya sauce, sesame oil and white pepper and stir to mix.

Fish Porridge

serves 4

Mama put chunks of carrots, tomatoes, onions and tender succulent pieces of fish with sesame oil and pepper in this sticky porridge. This mixture of ingredients resulted in the sweet, savoury, tangy fish porridge that I knew as a child. It was mind-blowingly good especially when she used new rice grains for the porridge and *ikan kurau* (threadfin) for its smooth, melt-in-the-mouth tenderness. New rice grains are the first harvest and are only available during certain months of the year. They cost slightly more but are worth every cent and can easily be bought at dry goods stalls in a wet market. Smell a handful of these grains: they have the most unbelievable fragrance, similar to the sweet intoxicating fragrance of pandan leaves. Needless to say, these grains make the best plain porridge. My stomach actually longs for a bowl of this understated porridge, especially during those periods of indulgent festive feasting.

Mama used *ikan bilis* (whitebait) stock to cook this porridge but I have substituted it with canned chicken broth. If you want to cook this using *ikan bilis* stock start by simmering 3 cups of *ikan bilis* (first washed under running water) with 8 cups of water for thirty minutes. Taste the porridge before adding any soy sauce as the *ikan bilis* stock can be quite salty.

1 cup new rice grains
400 g snapper, grouper
   or threadfin fillet
1 small carrot
1 medium onion
2 cups chicken stock
6 cups water
2 small tomatoes
Light soy sauce
Ground white pepper
Sesame oil
Ginger, cut into thin strips
Fried shallots
Coriander leaves

Peel the carrots and onions; cut them into bite-sized wedges. Put the carrots, onions, chicken broth and water in a big pot and bring to a boil. Meanwhile, wash and drain the rice. When the stock boils, lower the flame, add the rice, stirring to prevent the rice from sticking to the bottom of the pot. When the porridge starts to bubble, cover the pot and let it simmer gently for about 30 minutes until the vegetables are tender and the rice grains are very soft and sticky.

While the porridge is simmering, cut the tomatoes into wedges and prepare the fish by cutting it into small chunks. Set the tomatoes aside. Put all the fish into a bowl, cover with cling foil and leave it in the fridge.

Add the tomatoes to the porridge in the last 5 minutes of cooking time. When the porridge is done, turn off the flame and add the fish to it. Stir gently to separate the pieces of fish so that they will cook in the heat of the porridge. This way, the fish will remain tender and succulent. Once the fish pieces have turned opaque, the porridge is ready. Taste to check if any light soy sauce is needed. Ladle into bowls and top with white pepper, sesame oil, fried shallots, ginger strips and coriander sprigs.

Dried Shrimp Porridge

This is another one of Mama's tasty savoury porridges. Cooking porridge was definitely Mama's forte! This recipe uses ingredients like dried shrimps and dried baby whitebait that you can buy ahead and keep in the fridge. You can substitute the *ikan bilis* (whitebait) stock with a can of chicken stock and 6 cups of water. Baby anchovies are whole tiny fishes as shown in the picture.

1 cup new rice grains
2 cups split and boneless
   ikan bilis (whitebait)
1 chicken breast, skinned
8 cups water
¼ cup dried baby
   anchovies
2 teaspoons oil
¼ cup dried shrimps
2 cloves garlic
2 eggs, beaten
Light soy sauce (optional)
Fried shallots
Sesame oil
Ground white pepper
Spring onions, chopped

Put the *ikan bilis* in a sieve, wash them under running water and transfer them to a big pot. Cut the chicken breast into bite-sized pieces and add to the pot together with the 8 cups of water. Bring the contents to a boil, cover the pot and simmer for 30 minutes. In the meantime, wash and drain the rice. Next, put the dried baby anchovies in a sieve and wash them under running water; set aside. Wash the dried shrimps similarly. Mince the garlic.

When the stock has simmered for 30 minutes, top up with water to replace the volume lost to evaporation. Pour the stock through a sieve into another pot. Start the flame. Add the rice and dried anchovies to the stock. Stir occasionally to prevent the rice from sticking to the base. When the porridge starts to boil, lower the flame, cover the pot and simmer for half an hour.

In the meantime, heat the oil in a small pot and fry the dried shrimps for 5 minutes over a medium flame till the shrimps are thoroughly fried and very crispy. Stir occasionally. Add the garlic and continue to fry, stirring until the garlic browns. Add the fried shrimps and garlic to the porridge during the last ten minutes of cooking time.

Check if the porridge is too thick. If so, add some water and stir. Let the porridge bubble again before stirring in the beaten eggs. Turn off the flame and the porridge is ready to be served. Taste to check if it is necessary to add soy sauce. Ladle the porridge into bowls, top with the fried shallots, a few drops of sesame oil, some dashes of pepper and chopped spring onions.

Peanut Porridge

Mama's peanut porridge is a decidedly different kind from those sold at school canteens, hawker centres, food courts, or even Cantonese restaurants. It is chock-full of soft stewed peanuts while the fried cuttlefish strips and garlic make it very fragrant. It is a complete meal in itself with carbohydrates, protein and fibre. Mama always cooked extra as every one of us would go back for seconds. Baby anchovies are whole tiny fishes as shown on page 128.

½ cup raw peanuts,
   with skin
Water
2 cups split and boneless
   ikan bilis (whitebait)
¼ cup dried baby
   anchovies
¾ cup rice
½ cup dried cuttlefish
   strips
2 cloves garlic, minced
2 teaspoons oil
Light soy sauce (optional)
Fried shallots
Shallot oil
Chopped spring onions
Ground white pepper

Wash the peanuts, put them in a pot with 2 cups of water and bring it to a boil. Cover the pot, lower the heat and simmer for about 2 hours until the peanuts are very soft. Remember to top up the water to make up for that lost to evaporation.

Put the *ikan bilis* in a sieve and wash under running water. Bring the *ikan bilis* and 6 cups of water to boil in another pot. Cover the pot and simmer for 30 minutes. Strain the stock into a fresh pot.

When the peanuts are ready, wash and drain the rice. Wash the dried baby anchovies in a sieve under running water. Put the rice and baby anchovies into the *ikan bilis* stock. Add the peanuts and the water that they were cooked in. Bring everything to a boil, cover the pot and let it simmer for 30 minutes until the rice grains are very soft and broken up. Turn off the flame and let the porridge sit covered for 10 more minutes so it can soften further.

Now wash the cuttlefish strips and dry them on kitchen towels. Cut the strips if you find them too long. Heat the oil in a small pot or frying pan. When the oil is hot, fry the cuttlefish strips for about a minute before adding the minced garlic. Stir both these ingredients together until the garlic turns golden brown. Transfer to a little dish.

Before you serve the porridge, taste it to check if any light soy sauce is necessary. You can add a little more water if the porridge is too thick. Ladle the porridge into bowls, top with the fried cuttlefish strips, fried shallots, shallot oil, chopped spring onions and ground white pepper.

Simple Fried Rice

We often had this simple fried rice with 'overnight' rice, left over from dinner the day before. Usually there was only about a bowl of rice left over, so my sisters and I all clamoured for our share. Mama even had a story to go with it:

Long ago in China, there was a little boy who was ill-treated by his wicked stepmother. She would cook sumptuous meals for her own son but all her stepson had to eat was leftover fried rice with some lard. The poor boy devoured every grain hungrily and washed everything down with a cup of Chinese tea. Remarkably, the boy who ate all the seemingly good nutritious food remained thin. The other boy became plump, much to the utter bewilderment of the stepmother.

Of course, in today's context, we would be so envious of the thin boy's ability to eat abundantly yet remain fashionably slim, while shuddering at the thought of the cholesterol deposits in the plump boy's arteries. But I digress. This simple and tasty fried rice is cooked with just some oil, garlic, an egg and a splash of light soy sauce over a hot fire.

3 cups cooked rice
2 tablespoon oil
4 cloves garlic, peeled and smashed
2 eggs
4 teaspoons light soy sauce

Heat a non-stick wok well. Add the oil and garlic. Sauté until the garlic turns golden brown. Break the egg into the wok and scramble it with the wok fryer. Add the rice and fry until it is well coated with oil and thoroughly heated through. Add the light soy sauce. Stir well to mix the rice with the soy sauce. Transfer to a plate and enjoy.

Steamed Selar

Mama steamed fish for us almost daily. One of the easiest ways to prepare this dish is to steam the fish on its own, without even the addition of ginger or soy sauce. Fish cooked in this way has to be of the freshest quality. Just about any fish can be used but I chose to feature *selar* in this recipe as Mama favours this fish. Steam the *selar* on the day it is purchased. The fishmonger will gut the fish for you but remind him not to scale it so that you can peel off the skin in one piece when the fish is steamed.

The *selar* is eaten with a refreshing, delectable dip of chilli, garlic, calamansi lime juice and light soy sauce. This dip is at once spicy, tangy, fruity and salty. I can easily finish an entire fish by myself.

2 *selar* (Horse Mackerel), about 200 g each
2 red chilli padi, deseeded
1 clove garlic, minced
6 calamansi limes
4 teaspoons light soy sauce

Wash the *selar* well and dry them with kitchen towels. Place the *selar* on a dish that can fit into the steamer. Make sure the fish are at room temperature before steaming them.

Thinly slice the chilli padi. Divide the chillies and garlic between 2 sauce dishes. Halve the calamansi limes and remove all the seeds. Squeeze the juice directly into the sauce dishes. Add light soy sauce to the mix and give everything a stir. Now the dipping sauce is ready.

Heat the steamer. When steam starts to escape, put the fish into the steamer and cover immediately. Steam for 5 to 6 minutes over high heat. Serve the *selar* hot with the chilli-lime dip.

Prawn with Spring Onion

serves 4

We are very familiar with the use of diced spring onions as a garnish in soups and porridge but in this dish, it has a co-starring role. Other than imparting its sweetness, it also acts as a sponge, soaking up the aromatic oil and gravy. You won't look at spring onions in the same light again.

500 g medium prawns
16 stalks spring onions
1½ tablespoons oil
4 cloves garlic, finely sliced
4 teaspoons light soy sauce
2 tablespoons water

Shell the prawns and devein them; leave the tails on if you like. Wash the spring onions and shake off as much water as you can. Cut the spring onions, both green and white parts, into 5-centimetre lengths.

Heat the oil in a wok until it's very hot. Add the garlic and sauté until it turns golden brown. Add the spring onions, followed by the soy sauce. When the soy sauce contacts the hot wok and starts sizzling and evaporating, it will produce the most aromatic smell. This is what we want to capture in the dish. Let the soy sauce sizzle as you stir everything around for 2 to 3 seconds. Add the prawns, stir continuously for 2 to 3 more seconds before adding the water. Continue to stir as the prawns cook. Turn off the heat when the prawns lose all their raw colouring. Serve with rice.

Pan-fried Pork Chops

serves 4

This is another one of Mama's simple, easy-to-prepare dishes which she made when she was too tired to cook anything elaborate. Still, this dish is consummately delicious. It's a bit like a pork chop but without the mess of the egg-wash-and-breadcrumbs routine. The pork is simply seasoned with ingredients we all have in the kitchen and then pan-fried. So elementary, yet so good.

8 slices of pork loin,
  about ½ cm thick
¼ teaspoon ground white
  pepper
4 teaspoons corn flour
2 teaspoons superior dark
  soy sauce
2 teaspoons light soy sauce
Chinese lettuce leaves
Oil for frying

Pound each piece of pork with a meat tenderizer or a heavy granite pestle. Marinade with the pepper, corn flour, dark and light soy sauces. Place the lettuce in a single layer on a serving plate.

Heat 2 tablespoons of oil in a non-stick wok or frying pan. Fry 3 to 4 pieces of pork loin at a time for about half a minute on each side. Remove them from the wok and place on the lettuce leaves. Continue to fry the remaining pieces, using more oil if necessary. Serve with rice and a vegetable dish for a complete meal.

Hae Chor

PRAWN BALLS   makes about 35 balls

The very first time I tasted Teochew prawn balls or Hae Chor was at my Ah Gong's birthday dinner. I fell in love with them right away. Thereafter, whenever we attended any formal Chinese dinners, which wasn't often, I would eagerly look forward to the cold dish, hoping that Hae Chor would be one of the items served.

I remember that Papa once invited some visiting relatives from Hong Kong for dinner at our little flat in Joo Seng Road. That day, my parents spent every waking moment preparing and cooking for this special dinner. We only had a small dining table that comfortably sat four people, so Papa borrowed a big round table top and placed it on our table to accommodate the guests. My parents cooked many wonderful dishes for our special guests but the only dish I can recall is the Hae Chor. Mama even deep-fried dry bee hoon in hot oil so they puffed up into crispy munchies on which she placed her delicious golden Hae Chor. I remember eyeing that dish eagerly but children were not allowed any until the guests had eaten. When we finally got to eat, the deep-fried bee hoon weren't crispy anymore, and the Hae Chor was cold. Even then, I thought it was food fit for the gods.

Hae Chor, a Teochew specialty, is not commonly found in restaurants nowadays, though most restaurants serve a version similarly named. The Hae Chor mixture of prawns and pork is wrapped in bean curd skin, rolled up like a spring roll, steamed, and then deep-fried. In this original version, the meat mixture is shaped into balls and fried in the hot oil. It is the direct contact of the meat, specifically the prawns, with the oil that gives the Hae Chor its characteristic aroma and taste. They are so good on their own that it's unnecessary to serve them with any sauce. However, if you want a sauce to go with them, it has to be the sweet brown flour sauce that is also used in popiah (spring rolls). This is totally different from the dark sweet sauce used to fry char kuay teow. The two have distinctly different flavours, so make sure you get the right one.

350 g prawns

250 g minced pork

8 water chestnuts, peeled and diced

2 stalks spring onions, diced

1 large onion, chopped

1 tablespoon oyster sauce

2 teaspoons light soy sauce

½ teaspoon ground white pepper

1 tablespoon corn flour

Oil for deep frying

Lettuce leaves

Wash the prawns well. Shell, devein and dice the prawns coarsely. In a large mixing bowl, mix the prawns, pork, water chestnuts, spring onions, onions, cornflour and all the seasoning together.

Heat the oil in a small cooking pot. Shape the prawn and pork mixture into balls of about 2½ cm. Fry 6 to 8 prawn balls at a time until they are golden brown. Remove the fried prawn balls with a metal strainer and transfer them to a rack to drain off any excess oil. Fry the rest of the prawn balls. Arrange them on a bed of lettuce and serve.

Cabbage in Pork Gravy

serves 4

When Mama cooked braised pork (see page 85), she would save the gravy to cook a head of cabbage for us. The cabbage, slowly stewed in the gravy, was tender and sweet.

1 cabbage, about 500 g
1 cup braised pork gravy
4 cloves garlic, smashed
¼ teaspoon salt
Ground white pepper

Cut the cabbage into quarters. Wash under running water, separating the leaves slightly so the water can run between them. Cut off the core and cut each quarter into 2 pieces.

Put the cabbage, gravy, garlic, salt and pepper in a pot over high heat. Let it come to a boil then cover the pot. Lower the flame and let it simmer for about 15 minutes until the cabbage is tender.

Eggs with Pork Gravy

serves 2-3

Back when there weren't any refrigerators, we had something called a *kiam sng too*. *Kiam* refers to the dishes we typically ate with rice or porridge and *sng too* means ice cabinet although it was not a fridge by any stretch of the imagination. A *Kiam sng too* was actually a cabinet in which cooked dishes and/or leftover dishes were kept for the next meal. To ensure that leftover food didn't turn bad, Yee Mama brought unfinished soups or stews to the boil before keeping them. She would boil them again before serving them. Obviously Mama learned this from Yee Mama. Mama too didn't throw away any leftovers, not even braised pork gravy. In fact, we liked this scrambled eggs in braised pork gravy so much that Mama would deliberately make extra braised pork gravy so she could cook this dish the next day.

1 cup of braised pork gravy
3 eggs
Ground white pepper
1 teaspoon shallot oil
2 teaspoons fried shallots

Simply beat the eggs with a dash of white pepper. Heat up the braised pork gravy to a boil in a non-stick pot. Add a teaspoonful of shallot oil and the fried shallots for even more flavours. Lower the flame and pour the eggs in. Let the eggs cook over the gentle flame, stirring a couple of times, until they set. That's it! Eat this with plain porridge or rice. Heavenly!

Fish Cake Rolls

serves 4

Do you know that steamed fish cake rolls were once sold in cans? You won't find this kind of canned food anywhere in Singapore today, but all is not lost; Mama makes these egg rolls with fish paste that she buys from the market.

3 eggs
150 g fish paste
1½ tablespoon oil
Ground white pepper
1 stalk coriander leaves

First you need to make the omelette. Beat the eggs in a bowl. There is no need to add any salt or soy sauce to the eggs as the fish paste is quite salty. Heat the oil in a non-stick frying pan. Pour the eggs into the pan and spread them around to make an omelette of about 30-centimetres in diameter. Try to get as even a layer as possible. Fry until the omelette is cooked and the bottom is browned in patches.

Slide the omelette onto a cutting board. Let it cool while you fill the steamer with water and start heating it up.

Mix a few dashes of white pepper into the fish paste. Spread the fish paste evenly on the omelette all the way to the edge. Roll up the omelette. Transfer it to a plate and steam the egg roll for 10 minutes in the steamer. In the meantime, wash and cut the coriander leaves into short segments.

Cut the steamed roll diagonally into slices. Arrange the slices on a plate and garnish with the coriander leaves.

Soy Sauce Omelette

serves 4

This very delicious omelette is seasoned with dark soy sauce instead of just the usual light soy sauce. Being a burnt umber shade of brown, it is not exactly the prettiest of omelette, but don't let its appearance fool you. This omelette tastes much, much better than it looks.

4 eggs
2 teaspoons superior dark
   soy sauce
2 teaspoons light soy sauce
Ground white pepper
2 tablespoons oil

Beat the eggs together with the dark soy sauce, light soy sauce and dashes of white pepper. Heat the oil in a large frying pan and pour the eggs into the pan to make an omelette. Fry until the omelette is almost set before turning it over. You may cut the omelette into quarters and turn each quarter at a time. Fry the other side until it is set. It goes well with either porridge or rice.

Kailan with Eggs

serves 2

Mama can't recall where she learned to cook this dish. It is a little strange, marrying *kalian* with eggs, but it works.

200 g *kailan* (kale)
2 eggs
½ tablespoon light soy sauce
Ground white pepper
1 tablespoon oil
2 cloves garlic, minced
2 teaspoons oyster sauce
2 tablespoons water

Wash the *kailan* and shake off the excess water. Cut the leaves and stems into 2-centimetre lengths. Pare away the outer fibrous parts of the main stems and cut the stems diagonally into ½-centimetre thick slices. You should get about 6 cups of *kailan*.

Beat the eggs with the light soy sauce and dashes of white pepper. Set aside. Heat the oil in a wok; sauté the garlic until it turns golden brown. Add the *kailan* and stir to coat the vegetables with the oil. Add the oyster sauce and water; let the vegetables simmer for about a minute without reducing the flame. Add the eggs and let the eggs cook for a few seconds before stirring to scramble them. Once the eggs are set, the dish is done.

Chicken in Rice Wine

serves 2-3

Mama ate this dish frequently during her confinement period after childbirth. The sauce, full of the flavours of sesame oil, ginger and rice wine, goes spectacularly well with rice. You can use as much or as little ginger as you like; Mama would add a whole bowl of fine ginger strings. If you do not intend to eat the ginger, then use a thumb-size piece and slice it up instead of cutting it into thin strings so that it is easier to avoid eating them. I urge you to try the well-fried ginger strings as they are a highlight of this dish. I use young ginger here. It is only mildly hot and, when cut into such thin strings, it absorbs all that fragrant sesame oil and wine as it is being cooked. During Mama's confinement period, she ate nothing but meat cooked this way with rice. She only varied the kind of meat, using fish, pork or liver. The large amount of wine and ginger was believed to provide the warmth needed by the body after childbirth. If I had to eat the same thing everyday, then this dish wouldn't be a bad choice at all.

2 chicken legs
1 piece young ginger, half a
  palm size
4 cloves garlic
2 tablespoons sesame oil
¼ cup Chinese rice wine
2 teaspoons light soy sauce
1 tablespoon dark soy sauce
1 teaspoon sugar
¼ cup water

Remove the chicken skin if you wish. Cut each chicken leg into 4 pieces and rinse well, removing any bone chips. Cut the ginger into very thin strings. Finely mince the garlic.

Heat the sesame oil in a non-stick wok. Fry the ginger strings until they are golden; add the garlic and continue frying until both are golden brown. Include the chicken pieces, stirring to coat the chicken with oil. Now add the rice wine and stir to evaporate the alcohol. Mix in the light and dark soy sauces, the sugar and the water. Cover the wok and let the chicken simmer gently for about 30 minutes until it is tender; you will need to stir the chicken a couple of times and check if the sauce dries up too quickly. Add a little more water if it does. Serve immediately with rice.

Pork with Chinchalok

Pork with *chinchalok* (brined baby shrimps) was a dish Mama had clean forgotten about. I only remembered this exciting dish when I thought about the food we used to eat. It is just too good to be buried in the past. Using very common ingredients like shallots, chillies and *chinchalok*, it is very easy to cook.

250 g pork fillet
5 tablespoons *chinchalok*
   (brined baby shrimp)
20 shallots
2 cloves of garlic
2 red chillies
1 red *chilli padi*
   (bird's eye chilli)
1 stalk coriander leaves
2 teaspoons corn flour
¾ cup water
1½ tablespoons oil

Cut the pork fillet into thin slices about 3-millimetres thick. Slice each shallot into 4 to 5 pieces. Thinly slice the garlic and both types of chillies. Cut the coriander into 2-centimetre lengths. Mix the corn flour and water together.

Heat the oil in a non-stick wok and sauté the shallots, garlic and chillies for a few seconds. There is no need for the shallots or the garlic to brown. Add the *chinchalok* and fry for a few more seconds, followed by the corn flour and water mixture, stirring until the sauce starts to bubble. Add the pork fillet and stir continuously until the pork is cooked. Taste to check the seasoning. If it is not salty enough, add more *chinchalok* instead of salt. Transfer the pork to a serving dish; garnish with the coriander leaves and eat this with hot rice.

Hae Bee Hiahm

SPICY PRAWN FLOSS

makes 4 cups

When I was young, I categorized the food we ate into different groups: there was 'everyday food' like porridge and steamed fish; 'Sunday food' like Papa's prawn noodle soup and Sin Chew Bee Hoon; there was the 'special occasion food' like chicken curry and Hae Chor; and there was the 'once-in-a-blue-moon' food like Hae Bee Hiahm.

Cooking Hae Bee Hiahm in the past was a wickedly punishing task. Since there was no electric blender, everything had to be pounded by hand. It was therefore not surprising that Mama rarely cooked this dish, tasty as it might be. My sisters and I took turns helping Mama to do the pounding, and we would salivate with anticipation, taking in the incredibly intense, spicy, aromatic fragrance of the Hae Bee Hiahm as it was being fried. We always told Mama that she didn't have to cook any other dish; just make plenty of Hae Bee Hiahm as that was all we needed to eat with rice.

Instead of adding water to the ingredients to facilitate the grinding, I add oil. If the ground ingredients are too wet it will prolong the frying process as sufficient moisture has to evaporate in order to get a dry, well-fried Hae Bee Hiahm. Do make more Hae Bee Hiahm than you can eat; you can freeze the extra or give it away.

300 g dried shrimps
30 shallots, peeled
9 cloves of garlic, peeled
12 candlenuts
6 red chillies, deseeded
3 red *chilli padi* (bird's eye chilli), deseeded
½ tablespoon *belacan* (shrimp paste)
1½ cups oil
1 tablespoon sugar
Salt (optional)

Wash the dried shrimps in a colander under running water. Transfer them to a bowl and add ½ cup of water. Let the shrimps soak for about 20 minutes to absorb some of the water so that they will be easier to grind. Divide the shrimps into 2 or 3 portions and grind each portion finely in a blender. Remove and set aside.

Roughly cut up the shallots, garlic, candlenuts and both types of chillies into smaller pieces. Put all these ingredients, as well as the *belacan* in a blender. Add ½ cup of oil (from the 1½ cups) to get the blender going smoothly. Use the pulse button so you can better control the texture of the ground ingredients. You do not want a smooth puree. Use a chopstick to free any ingredients that may get caught below the blades.

To fry the Hae Bee Hiahm, heat a non-stick wok. Pour the remaining oil into the wok and let it heat up. Now add the ground spices and fry for about 5 minutes. Watch your fire: if bits of the shallots or chillies come popping out of the wok, the fire is too hot. Lower the flame and maintain the busy bubbling of the ingredients in the wok, stirring often.

After 5 minutes of frying, add the dried shrimps. Stir well to mix. The dried shrimps will be like a sponge and absorb the oil very quickly. Continue to stir and fry over a low to medium heat. You will need to fry this for about 20 minutes so that the moisture in the dried shrimps and spices can gradually evaporate. You have to stir every two to three minutes to ensure even frying as the Hae Bee Hiahm at the bottom of the wok will brown more quickly. As you fry, the colour of the Hae Bee Hiahm will turn increasingly darker: from a light orange to a deep reddish brown.

Lastly, add the sugar and stir to mix. Taste to check if any salt is needed according to your taste. You can transfer the Hae Bee Hiahm to another dish to cool or you can just let it cool in the wok.

When the Hae Bee Hiahm is completely cooled, store it in jars and keep it in the fridge if you can resist eating it with rice straight away!

Ghoh Sioh Oh

SWEET BRAISED YAM

Ghoh Sioh Oh is similar to Oh Nee (Yam Pudding, page 117), except that it is much easier and quicker to cook. The yam is thinly sliced and braised in a sweet syrup. When we were young, Mama didn't have the time to make Oh Nee but I do remember her cooking Ghoh Sioh Oh every now and then. We usually ate it with toothpicks, piercing each piece of tender yam, dipping it in the sweet sauce to make sure it was well coated before eating it.

Mama originally cooked Ghoh Sioh Oh without the addition of coconut. Later, she found that adding a bit of coconut greatly improves the taste of this dish. I use a couple of tablespoons of coconut powder for convenience.

1 small yam, about 600 g
2 shallots
2 pandan leaves
1 tablespoon oil
1 cup water
½ cup castor sugar
2 tablespoons coconut
    powder

Put on some gloves before handling the yam or you will get that intolerable itch from touching the raw yam with your bare hands. Peel the yam, wash it under running water and cut it into 4 or 6 segments as you would an orange. Slice each segment into ½ to 1-centimetre thick pieces. Peel the shallots and thinly slice them. Tie the pandan leaves into a knot.

Heat the oil in a non-stick wok and fry the shallot slices until they turn golden brown. Add the yam and stir to mix well. Now add all the water, sugar and pandan leaves and stir until the sugar dissolves. When the water comes to a boil, cover the wok tightly and lower the flame. Let the yam simmer for 15 to 20 minutes, stirring once or twice during the simmering process. As it cooks, a bit of the water will evaporate and the starch from the yam will thicken the water. This results in a thick, sweet gravy. Add a bit more water if it evaporates too fast.

When the yam is soft enough to be easily cut with a spoon, add the coconut powder and stir to mix well. Discard the pandan leaves and transfer the Ghoh Sioh Oh to a serving dish. Serve it hot.

Pandan Coconut Jelly

I can remember a period when Mama, my aunties and their friends were all into making *agar-agar*. There were all kinds: plain ones, those made with coconut milk, and even some with egg whites stirred in for a cloudy, marbled effect. Unlike the little *konnyaku* jellies we are accustomed to seeing nowadays, this pandan coconut *agar-agar* that Mama made was set in a big, beautiful jelly mould. She then turned it out onto a platter and brought the elegant dish to the table. I like *agar-agar* that is redolent with the fragrant taste of coconut and this pandan–coconut *agar-agar* definitely delivers that.

I use a 5-cup capacity jelly mould. This recipe is enough for one such mould with about an extra cup leftover. I pour the extra portion into a plastic container, which sets quite quickly in the fridge. This way I get to indulge in my cravings without having to wait for the big one to set. If you don't have a jelly mould, you can always use a round/square cake tin, any plastic container or even *konnyaku* jelly moulds.

FOR JELLY
100g pandan leaves
¾ – 1 cup water

FOR JELLY
1 packet *agar-agar* powder,
 12 g
4 pandan leaves
3¾ cups water
1¼ cups sugar
1 cup evaporated milk
1 cup coconut milk
¼ cup pandan juice
Green food colouring

To make the pandan juice, wash 100g of pandan leaves well. With your kitchen scissors, snip the leaves into 2-centimetre segments. Put all the cut leaves in a blender and add ¾ to 1 cup water to get the blender going. Grind the leaves well. Sieve the juice through a fine sieve into a container, squeezing out as much juice from the leaves as possible. Use 1 tablespoon for this recipe. The rest can be frozen in an ice-cube tray and used for making Nasi Lemak rice, *kueh* or cakes.

Put the *agar-agar* powder, water, sugar and pandan juice into a big pot. Tie the 4 pandan leaves into a knot and add this to the pot. Bring everything to a boil. Turn off the flame and discard the pandan leaves. Add the evaporated milk and coconut milk, and stir to mix well. Put in one or more drops of green food colouring into the mixture to obtain the desired shade of green. Ladle into the jelly mould and let the *agar-agar* cool completely.

Cover the *agar-agar* mould and refrigerate for at least 4 hours or overnight until it sets. When it Is ready to be served, turn out the *agar-agar* onto a plate. Slice and serve.

Roots & Wings

As I picture snapshots of past events, I can't help but experience a wave of nostalgia that is tinged with a measure of regret for the mindless and careless way I interacted with all the important people in my life, unaware that their lifestyle would one day be a thing of the past. Now, years later, I am moved by their routine work and the dedication with which they did them. I have a new-found admiration and respect for Hua Mama, Yee Mama, Ah Peh, Ah Mm, Ah Gou, Papa and Mama. If only I had cherished those moments more!

So much has changed in just one generation. Our food history has evolved in a startling way. As a child, I ate mainly Chinese food, but now we have a huge exposure to international fare: pasta, croissants, burgers, sushi, tom yum soup, tandoori chicken, kimchi – the list goes on. Although I find myself cooking such food with increasing frequency, I realise that we cannot afford to relinquish and forget the food of our parents and the generations before them.

I am so grateful that I learned to cook at a fairly young age. I learned about food preparation from observing the way Mama and Papa prepared ingredients for our meals. When I was about eight or nine, Mama let me help with the easy jobs like washing vegetables. I rather enjoyed washing vegetables as it was a chance to play with water, but I would squirm each time I came across a caterpillar hiding among the leafy greens – and this I experienced more frequently than I cared for. Peeling the paper-thin membrane of spinach stalks, scaling and gutting fish, cleaning squids, peeling prawns, slicing meat against the grain, cutting apples and oranges – all these I learned from watching Mama. Later she taught me how to season food and to marinate meats. When I was about thirteen, I was able to cook the dishes for an entire meal with Mama's guidance.

My fascination for cooking was also piqued by the trips to the wet market with Mama. The place was both riveting and revolting. I had to tread ever so carefully on the floor that was perpetually covered with dirty water that

pooled into puddles. I often wondered why the water was such a disgusting shade of black and where it came from in the first place. I had to fight visions of myself falling face-down into that muck. Pausing by the fruit stalls brought temporary relief as I was distracted by the sweet fragrance of the colourful fruits on display. Mama would look for the perfect, unblemished apple or orange, feeling its weight in her hand. I was not allowed to touch any of the fruits but I observed carefully as she took her time choosing them. To watch Mama buy ingredients and then turn them into delectable dishes was an engaging learning process.

Buying chicken was quite an adventure. We rarely ate chicken as it was relatively expensive compared to pork. When I was young, poultry didn't come in white styrofoam trays neatly wrapped with cling foil. The chicken stall was situated right in the middle of the market and was like a stage on which drama unfolded. One couldn't miss the squawking chickens which were crowded together in cages. There would be a flurry of feathers and louder squawks whenever

a hand reached into a cage and pulled out a protesting bird. Then came the scene that was so fascinating yet repulsive. I simply couldn't turn my eyes away. The doomed bird was held in the chicken seller's grip such that its neck was forced backward and its body immobilized. With the knife in his other hand, the chicken seller slit the chicken's throat, immediately turning the neck downward so that the steady stream of blood flowed into an aluminium container. All this was accomplished in an economy of time and movement with great professional flair. When the chicken had dripped dry, it was cast into a large cylindrical contraption and covered with a lid. The inside of this fascinating device would start spinning, much like a washing machine. When it stopped, the seller would lift out a stripped chicken, put it in a bag and hand it to the shopper – freshly slaughtered, still warm to the touch.

By the time I finished school, I was able to cook a fair number of dishes. I was the cook for a youth camp; I planned the entire menu with the help of a committee and cooked for all the campers. It was quite a scary but exhilarating experience for me to have all that responsibility. Cooking was left behind when I started work. It was not until years later,

after I had my children, that I started cooking again. My foray into Western food was a result

THIS PAGE: (Top) *Here I am in a clam-shaped cane chair popular in the Fifties; (Bottom) a chicken stripping machine in use.* FACING PAGE: *A homey kitchen with memories in every corner.*

of learning to cook spaghetti and chicken stew from a friend. It opened up a world of new ingredients I had never encountered before: tomato puree, extra-virgin olive oil and herbs like rosemary, thyme and tarragon. Browsing through cookbooks in the library was a most pleasurable time of learning as I salivated over

vivid pictures and insatiably read many recipes.

When I bought my own oven, it was just like acquiring a pair of wings. I was liberated and could go where I had never gone before in the kitchen. I could grill cheeses – it was pure magic watching the cheese melt into a gooey softness before turning golden brown. I could roast chickens – the first one I roasted was a tamarind chicken from a recipe I got from the newspaper. I was so excited that I invited relatives over for dinner without even knowing if the roast would turn out well. I could roast ribs, grill sausages and make *kaya-goo-you* toast (coconut jam and butter on toast). Best of all, I could bake cakes, cookies, pastries and bread – all my favourite things.

While embracing the cuisines of other cultures and exploring modern Chinese cuisine, I continue to cook the food of my parents and grandparents. I feel an enormous responsibility to preserve my culinary heritage and food history. I can see you reading these recipes and stories, probably over a leisurely cup of coffee, reflecting on the lives of my forefathers, deciding which recipe to try. I consider myself truly fortunate and blessed to be in this place and time, straddling the culinary worlds of past and present. There is so much to learn, so many recipes to cook and so many new ones to create. There is no better time to be for an enthusiastic cook.

Roast Turmeric Chicken

A roast chicken, whether presented whole or carved on a platter, topped with garnishes is so stunning and elegant. Those who have never roasted one before can be forgiven for assuming that it takes a great deal of culinary expertise to prepare it. Nothing is further from the truth. In fact, if you don't learn to cook anything else, learn to roast a chicken. It is easy and so sure to impress.

Roasting a chicken in a very hot oven for a shorter time produces a more moist bird as opposed to a longer cooking time in a moderately hot oven. I also prefer a smaller chicken of roughly 1 kilogram as the proportion of seasoning and skin to meat is just about right. When I am feeding more people, I'll roast two such chickens rather than a single large one. I just need to increase the roasting time by 10 to 15 minutes. An important point to remember is that the chickens must be at room temperature before you start the roasting.

I am very fond of fried chicken pieces, a specialty found in Malay food stalls. The salt and turmeric marinade makes the chicken fragrant and gives it a very attractive deep yellow hue. I toyed with the idea of roasting a chicken with these very same seasonings. And surely it wouldn't hurt to add some garlic? However, garlic burns quite fast and easily, so I put it under the chicken skin. This way, the flavour of the garlic permeates the entire chicken. The garlic also imparts moisture to the meat, resulting in a tender, and succulent chicken. Mama in particular, simply loves chicken that I roast in this way.

1 chicken, about 1 – 1.2 kg
6 large cloves of garlic
2 teaspoons salt
5 teaspoons turmeric powder
1 stalk spring onions
1 red chilli
1 stalk of coriander leaves
½ cucumber

Line a roasting tin or tray big enough to hold the chicken with aluminium foil, then with non-stick baking paper. The non-stick baking paper will prevent the skin of the roasted chicken from being stuck to the foil. Remove the neck and feet of the chicken. Wash the chicken well, then drain and dry thoroughly with kitchen towels. Place the chicken on a large plate.

Peel the garlic and pound it with 1 teaspoon of the salt into a fine paste. Add 2 teaspoons of the turmeric powder to the garlic paste and mix well. Divide the paste into 6 parts.

With your fingers, carefully separate the chicken skin from the flesh, one side of the chicken at a time. Start from the neck end and work your way from the right ride of the breast to the thigh, then the drumstick. Be careful not to rip off the skin or make any holes in it. Do the same with the other side of the chicken. Take one portion of the garlic paste and push it under the skin all the way to the drumstick and spread it as evenly as possible all over it. Take another portion of garlic paste, this time pushing it under the skin and smear it over the thigh. Next, spread the third portion of garlic paste under the skin and over the breast. Repeat with the remaining 3 portions of garlic paste on the other half of the chicken.

Rub the remaining teaspoon of salt all over the skin, making sure to pay particular attention to the wings which have not been salted under the skin. Lastly, spread the remaining turmeric powder all over the chicken, covering every part well. Tuck the tips of the wings below the chicken. Now transfer the chicken to the prepared tin, breast side up. Leave the chicken to marinade for at least 2 hours. If you are roasting the chicken the next day, wrap the tin tightly with aluminium foil and keep the chicken in the fridge. Bring the chicken out well in advance (at least 5 hours) so it can return to room temperature before roasting.

Preheat the oven to 240 degrees Celsius. Roast the chicken uncovered for 30 minutes. Check midway through the cooking process. If the chicken is browning too quickly, cover it very loosely with a piece of foil. Once the chicken has been roasted for 30 minutes, remove it from the oven. Let it rest for at least 20 minutes before cutting.

While the chicken is roasting, you can prepare the garnishes. Slice the spring onions diagonally into long thin strips. Do the same with the chilli after removing the seeds. Soak both the spring onion and chilli strips in a bowl of water so that the strips will curl attractively. Cut the stalk of coriander leaves into short segments. Peel and thinly slice the cucumber.

When you are ready to cut the chicken, hold it up vertically so all the juice in the cavity can flow out into the roasting tin. Cut the chicken and arrange the pieces skin side up on a platter. Pour all the chicken juices from the roasting tin into a bowl. Skim off the fat on top, then pour this juice all over the cut chicken. Arrange the cucumber slices around the chicken. Dry the spring onion and chilli strips on kitchen towels and pile these as well as the coriander leaf on the chicken.

Rice Wine Chicken Soup

Even though it is supposedly health fortifying, I am not used to drinking Chinese rice wine. Instead, I use the rice wine in cooking, as it lends a wonderful flavour to soups and chicken dishes. This soup is actually the result of a failed recipe for drunken chicken. To avoid wasting the ingredients, I decided to throw all the chicken pieces, wine and soy sauce together with some sugar and sesame oil into a pot. I then added water and boiled the whole lot to make soup. And guess what? The soup tasted unbelievably satisfying.

You can make this soup with chicken bones that can be easily purchased from supermarkets or wet markets. My proportion for making chicken soup is one chicken carcass to one cup of water for one serving. I use only half a tablespoon of rice wine for one serving of soup as I don't want an overpowering taste of wine. At the same time I want this soup to be palatable for small children. Of course I won't stop you from increasing the quantity of wine for a stronger flavour. However, you may need to add a bit more sugar and salt to temper the tartness of the wine.

4 chicken carcasses
2 teaspoons sugar
4 cups water
2 tablespoons Chinese rice wine
¾ teaspoon salt
4 cloves garlic, smashed
2 teaspoons sesame oil

Cut up the chicken carcasess into smaller pieces. Put all the ingredients into a pot and bring to a boil. Cover the pot and let it simmer for an hour. Don't worry about the scum that rises to the top at this stage. When the soup has simmered for an hour, top it up with water to make up for the amount lost to evaporation. Pour the stock through a sieve into another pot to effectively rid the soup stock of all the scum. Ladle the soup into bowls and enjoy!

If you want to serve the soup with chicken in it, then add 2 chicken legs cut into bite-size pieces into the strained soup. Bring to a boil, cover the pot and let it simmer very gently for about 20 to 30 minutes until the chicken is tender. Adjust the seasoning and serve.

*

Porridge can be made from this wonderful stock. You will need 2 cups of this soup to a scant ¼ cup of rice grains for 1 serving of porridge. Just add some shredded chicken, ginger strips, diced spring onions, pepper and sesame oil and you'll have a bowl of tasty porridge.

Chinchalok Omelette

I discovered this omelette in a small, unadorned Peranakan restaurant in Malacca and loved it immediately. It is dissimilar to the Fu Yong Tan (Egg Fu Yong) from *zhi char* stalls. Fu Yong Tan is fried until it is golden brown and crispy around the edges, but this *chinchalok* omelette is only lightly fried, with just a slight golden colouring here and there. There is no need to add any salt or soy sauce to the eggs as the *chinchalok* is very salty.

2 eggs
1 teaspoon *chinchalok*
  (brined baby shrimp)
1 stalk coriander leaves
1 red chilli
1 tablespoon oil

Wash the coriander leaves and cut them into short segments. Thinly slice the red chilli. Beat the eggs and *chinchalok* together. Heat the oil in a non-stick wok and pour the egg mixture into it. Let the eggs fry until it is set on the bottom. Turn the omelette over to the other side and continue to fry until the other side is set. Transfer the omelette to a plate and pile the coriander leaves and chilli slices on top.

Dory With Curry Leaves

It is amazing that now we can get fish like halibut, cod, salmon and pacific dory, which were virtually unheard of back when I was a child. With the exception of cod, the other fish are relatively inexpensive. Pacific dory is very affordable, so this is a fish we eat often. Because it is rather bland-tasting, a thoughtful creative marinade is required to transform it into a scrumptiously succulent treat.

3 pieces pacific dory fillet,
  about 300 g each
1 tablespoon corn flour
1 tablespoon oyster sauce
½ teaspoon superior dark
  soy sauce
1 tablespoon light soy
  sauce
4 teaspoons coarsely
  ground black pepper
6 stalks curry leaves
½ cup oil
1 cup flour

If you are using frozen fillets, thaw them first, then drain the fish well. Dry them with kitchen towels. Cut each fillet into 3 or 4 smaller pieces. Mix the corn flour, oyster sauce, light and dark soy sauces as well as the ground black pepper and curry leaves into a paste. Coat both sides of the fillets well with the marinade and set them aside for 30 minutes.

Heat the oil in a non-stick pot or frying pan. Remove the curry leaves from the fish. Dredge 2 to 3 pieces of fillet with the flour. Put them in a large sieve and shake them around gently to get rid of any excess flour. Make sure you have a container to hold the excess flour; a piece of cling foil or aluminium foil would do just as well. Repeat for the remaining fish.

Fry 2 or 3 fillets in hot oil for about a minute on each side until they are brown. Remove the fried fish from the oil and drain on a rack. Fry the remaining pieces in the same way. Serve the fried dory immediately while they are hot and crispy. I don't think these fillets need any accompanying sauces but, if you like, you can serve them with mayonnaise or wedges of lemon.

Garlic Wings

There may seem to be a copious quantity of garlic in this recipe but, if you reduce the amount, what would be the point? 'Garlic' is the operative word here, so go for the bigger and juicier cloves. I use mixed herbs but a combination of just rosemary and thyme works as well. You can even use rosemary on it's own but use only 1 teaspoon as it is quite strong-tasting.

 I use a 2-kilogram packet of chicken wings, which works out to about 18 wings. First, I defrost the wings a day before (this takes the better part of a day or night). Just leave the whole bag in the sink before you go to bed. Deal with the wings in the morning and put the marinated lot into the fridge until you are ready to roast them.

2 kg chicken wings
8 cloves garlic, finely
 grated
2 teaspoons salt
1 tablespoon ground black
 pepper
½ cup corn flour
2 teaspoons mixed herbs
Slices of lemon or lime

Wash and drain the chicken wings well. Marinade them with the salt, ground black pepper, corn flour, mixed herbs and grated garlic. Use your hands to mix and rub the marinade evenly all over the wings. Cover the wings and leave them in the fridge for at least two hours.

Preheat the oven to 240 degrees Celsius or 220 degrees if it is a fan-assisted oven. Line a baking tray with foil, then with non-stick baking paper. The non-stick baking paper is essential to prevent the wings from sticking to the foil. You may have to roast the wings in 2 or 3 batches, depending on the size of the oven and your tray.

Take the wings out of the oven now. The wings will be roasted for a total of 30 minutes to crisp the skin. Chilling them well will ensure that they won't overcook. Arrange the wings on the tray, leaving just a little space between them. Roast the wings for 15 minutes, then turn them over and roast for another 15 minutes. Repeat for the remaining wings.

Transfer all the roasted wings to a serving platter and serve with slices of lemon or lime.

Index